CHANGING ADMINISTRATIONS

CHANGING

ADMINISTRATIONS

The 1961 and 1964 Transitions
in Six Departments

DAVID T. STANLEY

THE BROOKINGS INSTITUTION
Washington, D. C.

© 1965 by

THE BROOKINGS INSTITUTION
1775 Massachusetts Avenue, N.W., Washington, D. C.

Published November 1965
Library of Congress Catalogue Card Number 65-28725

THE BROOKINGS INSTITUTION is an independent organization devoted to nonpartisan research, education, and publication in economics, government, foreign policy, and the social sciences generally. Its principal purposes are to aid in the development of sound public policies and to promote public understanding of issues of national importance.

The Institution was founded December 8, 1927, to merge the activities of the Institute for Government Research, founded in 1916, the Institute of Economics, founded in 1922, and the Robert Brookings Graduate School of Economics and Government, founded in 1924.

The general administration of the Institution is the responsibility of a self-perpetuating Board of Trustees. The trustees are likewise charged with maintaining the independence of the staff and fostering the most favorable conditions for creative research and education. The immediate direction of the policies, program, and staff of the Institution is vested in the President, assisted by the division directors and an advisory council, chosen from the professional staff of the Institution.

In publishing a study, the Institution presents it as a competent treatment of a subject worthy of public consideration. The interpretations and conclusions in such publications are those of the author or authors and do not purport to represent the views of the other staff members, officers, or trustees of the Brookings Institution.

Foreword

THIS VOLUME IS ONE of Brookings' studies of the transfer of power and of continuity of administration in the federal government. Laurin L. Henry's *Presidential Transitions* (1960) analyzed the Taft-Wilson, Wilson-Harding, Hoover-Roosevelt, and Truman-Eisenhower transitions. Mr. Henry extended this work to include the Eisenhower-Kennedy transition in two papers in *The Presidential Election and Transition 1960-1961* (Paul T. David, ed., 1961): "The Transition: Transfer of Presidential Responsibility" and "The Transition: The New Administration." These analyses of the take-over process concentrated on the overall performance of the new President and his associates.

Two other Brookings publications give the personal perspectives of performers in the drama of transition: *The Job of the Federal Executive,* by Marver Bernstein (1958), and *The Assistant Secretaries,* by Dean E. Mann with Jameson W. Doig (1965).

The present study concentrates on the more detailed problems of the transfer of responsibility in the early sixties in six federal organizations: the Departments of State; Defense; Interior; Agriculture; Health, Education, and Welfare; and the Federal Aviation Agency. Initial research consisted of interviews with officials conducted in 1961 by Mr. Henry, James R. Klonoski, Mr. Mann, Burton Sapin, and John Schott. Mr. Henry planned and coordinated this work. In 1964-1965 David T. Stanley conducted a few follow-up interviews in each of the departments, analyzed the earlier interview notes, brought the research up to date in other ways, and wrote the manuscript. The study was conducted under the supervision of George A. Graham, Director of Governmental Studies. Miss Deborah H. Bliss served as research assistant and secretary.

Portions of the draft manuscript were read and commented upon by officials of the departments concerned and by Clarence H. Danhof, Joseph L. Fisher, H. Field Haviland, Jr., Marian D. Irish, Charles B. Saunders, Jr., Arthur Schlesinger, Jr., and George W. Wright. The entire draft benefited from the criticisms of a reading committee consisting of Laurin Henry, Roger W. Jones, and Wallace S. Sayre. The contributions of all these persons are gratefully acknowledged.

The Institution appreciates the support of the Carnegie Corporation, which financed a portion of the project.

The manuscript was edited by Frances M. Shattuck and indexed by Helen B. Eisenhart.

The author is responsible for the accuracy and appropriateness of the statements and interpretations. The views expressed in this book do not purport to represent those of the Carnegie Corporation, other staff members, officers, or trustees of the Brookings Institution.

Robert D. Calkins
President

August 1965
Washington, D. C.

Contents

ix

CHANGING ADMINISTRATIONS

1 / INTRODUCTION

The Change in the Presidency, 1961

> . . . During the last sixty days, I have been engaged in
> the task of constructing an Administration. It has been a
> long and deliberate process. Some have counseled greater
> speed. Others have counseled more expedient tests. . . .
>
> —President Kennedy
> Speech to the Massachusetts
> State Legislature, January 9, 1961[1]

W HEN PRESIDENT John Fitzgerald Kennedy delivered his inaugural address that bright and chilly noon of January 20, 1961, he was already well along in the task of taking over the government. Most department and agency heads had been appointed, and the subcabinet was nearly filled. Many policy guidelines had been laid down, and the desks of the new team were piled with reports from expert task forces and from career staff members. The new appointees had already been briefed by their principal subordinates.

The general story of the Kennedy take-over has been well told in Laurin Henry's two papers[2] and need not be told again. The reader may be helped, however, by a quick review of the background of the transition before the process in each of the six departments is discussed.

[1] John F. Kennedy, *To Turn the Tide* (Harper & Brothers, 1962), p. 4.
[2] Laurin L. Henry, "The Transition: Transfer of Presidential Responsibility" and "The Transition: The New Administration" in Paul T. David (ed.), *The Presidential Election and Transition 1960–1961* (Brookings Institution, 1961), pp. 205–67.

1

Current Events

The march of events in the nation and the world did not mark time waiting for this change of administration. It continued to put increased and often unexpected pressures upon the new administration and upon the departments studied in this book. Newspapers for the days just before the 1961 inauguration gave primary attention to President Eisenhower's valedictory (in which he warned of the power of the "military-industrial complex") and to preparations for the new administration. Yet they also reported:

> Intensification of "Hate U.S." policies in Cuba, following the breaking of diplomatic relations;
>
> Lowered morale of overseas troops because of curtailed travel of their dependents—at a time when they should have been primarily alert to other problems;
>
> B-52 bombers in the air twenty-four hours a day;
>
> Investigation of a catastrophic airline collision above New York City;
>
> Plans for joint development with Canada of Columbia River Basin resources;
>
> A 52 percent increase in school enrollments in ten years.

Thus the Kennedy administration, like any new administration, was moving into a highly dynamic situation.

Active, Yet Cautious Preparations

If national and world events were not waiting for the Kennedy administration, neither was the administration waiting for events to chart its course. The theme of "movement", of vigor, of activity, had carried over from the campaign without perceptible loss of momentum. The President-elect enjoyed only a few days of recreation before he began seeing callers from early morning till late at night, mainly about jobs to be filled and policies to be developed. Meanwhile many of his associates were also putting in countless hours of overtime.

The Talent Hunt

Much of this energy was devoted to discovering and sifting prospects for the hundreds of cabinet, subcabinet, and independent agency jobs that a President must fill. Leaders in this recruitment effort were the President-elect's brother, Robert F. Kennedy, who had run his campaign, and his brother-in-law, R. Sargent Shriver, later to become Director of the Peace Corps and still later chief of President Johnson's anti-poverty program. Robert Kennedy, assisted by the President-elect's aides Lawrence O'Brien, Richard Donahue, and Ralph Dungan, worked mainly through the political network developed during the campaign. Shriver, along with Adam Yarmolinsky and Harris Wofford, lawyers who had helped in the campaign, concentrated on the business, professional, and university worlds. A number of volunteer consultants worked on locating and evaluating prospects for particular departments or functions.[3] After a department head was selected, talent hunt recruiters worked with him to suggest names for jobs in that department and to evaluate other candidates.

Throughout this process the evaluations of candidates emphasized qualifications for the job, political acceptability, and such qualities as "judgment," "toughness," "integrity," "ability to work with others," "industry," and "devotion to the principles of the President-elect." The recruiters tried to find the ablest people in the nation, but inevitably compromises were made with quality because of time pressures, the sheer volume of the task, and political necessities.[4] Although the decision of the department head was generally the controlling factor, an analysis of the principal participants in the selection of political executives showed more White House influence in selections in the Kennedy administration than in the Truman and Eisenhower administrations.[5]

Studies and Briefings

Even before the election, studies had begun of problems to be faced by the incoming administration.

[3] *Ibid.*, pp. 218–23. See also Adam Yarmolinsky, "The Kennedy Talent Hunt," *The Reporter*, Vol. 24 (June 8, 1961), pp. 22–25; and Dean E. Mann with Jameson W. Doig, *The Assistant Secretaries* (Brookings Institution, 1965), pp. 72–73.

[4] Henry, *op. cit.*, p. 219.

[5] Mann, *op. cit.*, p. 88.

BROOKINGS MEMOS AND MEETINGS. In the summer of 1960 the Brookings Institution began efforts to focus the attention of both presidential candidates and their associates upon problems to be faced in assuming power. Memoranda were prepared discussing the most urgent matters to be dealt with by the President-elect: actions to be taken between election and inauguration; organization of the White House staff and the Executive Office; relationships with Congress; reorganization authority; the cabinet; press relations; foreign affairs; the Bureau of the Budget; personnel problems; and the independent regulatory commissions.

These papers were discussed in September and October 1960 at meetings of an advisory committee of distinguished citizens of both political parties, all of whom had held important federal posts.[6] Observers representing both presidential candidates and the White House also attended. President-elect Kennedy later received a full set of the memoranda after they had been revised on the basis of the discussions.

A series of reports was also prepared by a management consulting firm for the incoming heads of sixteen departments and major agencies. These documents listed the key positions to be filled and discussed some of the principal problems of organization and management to be faced by the new administrators.

THE TASK FORCES. President-elect Kennedy set up expert "task forces" to study the more important substantive problems confronting his administration. Twenty-nine such groups were enumerated by *Congressional Quarterly,* seven of them appointed before the election.[7] These studies put hundreds of talented people to work on basic problems facing the nation. They sum-

---

[6] Robert D. Murphy, Chairman, David K. E. Bruce, John J. Corson, Robert Cutler, Marion B. Folsom, William C. Foster, Henry H. Fowler, Gabriel Hauge, C. D. Jackson, James R. Killian, Jr., Charles S. Murphy, Frank Pace, Jr., James H. Rowe, Jr., and James E. Webb.

[7] "Pre-Inaugural Task Forces Unprecedented in History," *Congressional Quarterly Weekly Report,* Vol. 19 (April 7, 1961), pp. 620–23. See also Henry, *op. cit.,* pp. 216–18. The topics covered included: foreign policy, the national defense establishment, national security, natural resources, wheat, cotton, overseas food programs, regulatory agencies, Africa, Department of State, U. S. Information Agency, disarmament, balance of payments, foreign economic policy, U. S. information programs, depressed areas, exchange of persons, India, Latin America, space programs, American economy, education, health and social security, housing and

marized the issues for the President-elect and evaluated alternative courses of action. Of equal importance, they provided an opportunity for Mr. Kennedy and his immediate staff to appraise the capacities of task force members for federal jobs. As a further major advantage, members actually chosen for jobs got a running start on their work.[8] Task force reports influenced the policies and legislative programs of all six of the departments covered in this book, as later chapters will show.

Help from the Old Administration and the Career Staffs

Immediately after the election President Eisenhower congratulated Senator Kennedy and offered assistance in preparing for the change of administration. He designated his assistant, General Wilton Persons, as the person to handle liaison arrangements. Kennedy responded appreciatively and appointed Clark Clifford (who had taken part in the Brookings discussions) as his liaison representative. Clifford and Persons began meetings within a week. Kennedy met personally with Eisenhower on December 6 and again on January 19. Throughout the election-to-inauguration period both parties to the transition displayed a constructive and cooperative spirit. Both made it clear that, despite the extensive consultations and exchanges of information, the Eisenhower administration had full and sole executive responsibility until January 20.

Long before the election career officials had begun preparations for the change. The Bureau of the Budget provided the President-elect with briefing memoranda, and similar papers were developed throughout the departments and agencies for use of the new political executives. Limited office space and secretarial services were given to the incoming executives while they dealt with problems of program orientation and staff selection.[9]

---

urban development, tax policy, Peace Corps, economic policy, agriculture (overall), and feed grains.

[8] "Pre-Inaugural Task Forces," in *Congressional Quarterly Weekly Report*, p. 621.

[9] See Henry, *op. cit.*, pp. 205–34, for a fuller discussion of all these events.

Change at the Departmental Level

In general, then, the Kennedy administration was well and cooperatively prepared for its assumption of responsibility. How soon, how thoroughly, how smoothly it really began to "operate" at the departmental level are the main questions explored in this book. The initial transition to the Johnson administration in each department is also discussed briefly, but the 1963-64 transition produced few changes in policies or in people. The real character and direction of the Johnson presidency did not emerge clearly until after his reelection. Most of the changes that took place as the New Frontier became the Great Society make up another story, one beyond the scope of this book.

A Model Pattern Imagined

If one were to develop a model (or perhaps stereotype) of the process of change in a federal department after a party change in the presidency, it might look something like this:

Voters elect a president of a different party, thus implicitly endorsing his policies.

President selects a secretary in sympathy with these policies and reasonably qualified to direct the functions of the department.

Secretary-designate (with more help than he can use and less than he really needs) puts together a team of assistant secretaries and confidential, policy-determining assistants.

This new team is offered briefings and material from the outgoing team, who are depressed by the election results, preoccupied with their own futures, and inclined to postpone major decisions.

Key career staff members also offer orientation and indicate cooperation; the new team accepts but wonders how far their loyalty and competence can be trusted.

All sorts of pressures from legislators, interest groups, and citizens are brought to bear on the new department head and his staff.

The new secretary and his team prepare a legislative program and a revised budget to carry out their policies and start "selling" them to congressional leaders and constituency groups.

Changes are made in departmental organization, personnel, and procedures to put the new policies and programs into effect.

Variations Expected

The actual patterns of change among the five departments and one independent agency [10] selected for study varied greatly according to each organization's mission, its history, its current problems, its constituency relationships, its internal organization and bureaucratic mores, the interplay of the personalities and capacities of new and old personnel, and what has been called "the quality of the political leadership of the moment, plus an element of sheer luck in regard to the circumstances of the times."[11]

These greatly varied patterns, however, have common threads: personnel problems, organizational change, legislative relationships, executive leadership. These will be commented upon in the final chapter after each departmental experience is examined in some detail.

[10] The reader will already have observed that all six are called "departments" for convenience.

[11] Henry, *op. cit.*, p. 267.

2

THE DEPARTMENT OF STATE
Old Hands, New Motive Power

> . . . we must sharpen our political and diplomatic tools—
> the means of cooperation and agreement upon which an
> enforceable world order must ultimately rest.
>
> —President Kennedy
> State of the Union Message,
> January 29, 1961

WHEN PRESIDENT-ELECT Kennedy an-
nounced his choice of Dean Rusk for Secretary of State on
December 12, 1960, the reaction of the public and of foreign
policy commentators was favorable. Not only had Rusk presided
over the far-flung good works of the Rockefeller Foundation, but
he was an "old hand" at the Department of State.[1] During the
Truman administration he had served as Assistant Secretary for
United Nations Affairs, Deputy Under Secretary, and Assistant
Secretary for Far Eastern Affairs.

Other well-qualified men soon joined the team. Chester Bowles,
the Under Secretary, had been a congressman, Governor of Connecticut, and Ambassador to India and Nepal. George Ball,
Under Secretary for Economic Affairs, had supervised the work
of six pre-inauguration task forces dealing with foreign policy and
with the Department of State. Most of the assistant secretaries
had held federal career jobs dealing with international relations
or seemed well prepared through other experience.

---

[1] This chapter on the Department of State deals with the "department proper,"
not including the Agency for International Development, the Peace Corps, the
U. S. Arms Control and Disarmament Agency, and the U. S. Information Agency.

Problems, Continuing Policies, Commitments

This team was facing problems of foreign policy that would severely test all its skills and knowledge, as well as those of the White House leadership.

Relations with the Soviet Union had settled back into the familiar pattern of world-wide pressures and counter-pressures, following the spectacular rupture after the U-2 incident in the middle of 1960. Chairman Khrushchev had expressed a wish to meet with the President-elect. There was armed conflict in the Congo, and the United Nations General Assembly could not agree on the role or degree of support of the U.N. peacekeeping troops there. Another civil war was being fought in Laos with the aid of both Soviet and Western arms and ideas. In Cuba Fidel Castro, now in power two years, continued to denounce the United States and to encourage subversion in other Latin American countries. In Europe Russian pressure to get the Western allies out of Berlin continued. Strains were apparent within the NATO alliance.

It was clear at the start that there would not be changes in the major *direction* of American foreign policy. Analysts who studied the public commitments of the new administration could discern differences in emphasis, in intended vigor of action, in personal touch or style, but not in basic policy.

The Democratic platform and campaign of 1960 had stressed the need for planning controlled disarmament, improving relationships with the other NATO powers, strengthening support of the United Nations, encouraging and aiding nonaligned underdeveloped countries, continuing firmness in defense of Berlin and Formosa, opposing admission of Communist China to the U.N., and for other steps to continue and develop, but not to change, major foreign policies. It would be difficult to select the respects in which the intended Kennedy approach was most different from the Eisenhower approach. Perhaps two would qualify: (1) a more vigorous foreign aid program, including reavowal of the Good Neighbor policy toward Latin American countries and a stronger helping hand to the new African nations; and (2) a strong, sustained effort toward nuclear disarmament, such as resulted in the 1963 test ban treaty.

Learning, Planning, Getting Started

The principal means by which the administration-to-be tried to think through its foreign policy problems and prepare some of its men to deal with them were the task forces mentioned in the previous chapter.

Task Forces on Foreign Policy

THE BALL-SHARON GROUP. On July 29, 1960, Mr. Kennedy asked Adlai Stevenson to prepare a report on foreign policy matters to be decided and acted upon. Stevenson, working with the aid of Washington lawyers George Ball and John Sharon, finished the report (which was never made public) and submitted it on November 14. Ten days later Kennedy asked Ball and Sharon to arrange for the preparation by task forces of more specific reports. Six of these were assigned, and all were completed before Inauguration Day. About 100 consultants in all contributed to these projects,[2] which dealt with:

Policies and personnel for relations with the countries of Africa
The Department of State itself (a partial summary stressed an expanded function for ambassadors)
Function, standing, organizational relationships, and key personnel of the United States Information Agency
Organization and policy formulation on disarmament
Balance of payments
Foreign economic policy

Several of the men involved in this work later took important posts in the Kennedy administration: Ball himself; Harlan Cleveland (Assistant Secretary of State for International Organization Affairs); Edward R. Murrow (Director, U. S. Information Agency); Paul H. Nitze (Assistant Secretary of Defense for International Security Affairs, and later Secretary of the Navy); Robert V. Roosa (Under Secretary of the Treasury for Monetary Affairs); George S. Springsteen (assistant to Ball); J. Kenneth Galbraith

[2] "Pre-Inaugural Task Forces Unprecedented in History," *Congressional Quarterly Weekly Report*, Vol. 19 (April 7, 1961), pp. 620–22.

(Ambassador to India); and Walt W. Rostow (Deputy Special Assistant to the President for National Security Affairs, and later Counselor and Chairman of the Policy Planning Council of the Department of State).

The people who served as consultants to these groups received no compensation. Expenses totaled about $25,000, of which about three-fourths was financed by foundation grants and about one-fourth by Ball personally. One of the organizers estimated the value of the donated services at $250,000.

The Ball-Sharon task forces were helped by three staff men loaned by the Department of State but otherwise received no significant government aid. Department officials were allowed to talk to members and staffs of the task forces, but the latter did not have access to government records.

Kennedy also asked the Ball-Sharon group to list possible candidates for top foreign policy jobs. They did so—"two pages of Democrats and one page of Republicans," according to one source —and many of these people were in fact appointed. Coordination with the Shriver "talent hunt" mentioned in Chapter 1 was easy because Adam Yarmolinsky, one of the hunters, was a former law associate of Ball and Sharon.

THE SORENSEN GROUP. Meanwhile another group of task forces, a few of them concerned with foreign policy, were working under the general supervision of Theodore Sorensen of Kennedy's staff. There was an early problem of coordination between the two groups. One of Kennedy's staff, fearing overlapping work, asked the Ball-Sharon group to suspend operations on two studies. Kennedy himself then saw to it that a satisfactory division of responsibility was worked out.

The Sorensen groups were working on these matters of interest to the Department of State:

United States information programs
Exchange of persons
India
Latin America
Peace Corps

As in the case of the Ball-Sharon group, all reports were turned in before the inauguration.

Of all these task force reports, only those on exchange of persons and on the Peace Corps were made public in full, although partial summaries of most of the others were released. The reports were intended mainly to be confidential guides to policy formulation, not public documents.

The task forces, then, were valuable both as a means of training and as aids to selection. These values declined rapidly, of course, as members of the new team arrived and began grappling with tangible problems of policy and administration. These values also were appreciated mainly by the incoming political executives. Some of the career staff, possibly defensive about policies they had helped develop, criticized the task force reports as not factual or realistic.

Briefings and Preliminary Contacts

Both the new and the old State teams were ambivalent about the extent to which the incoming group should be informed and involved. Secretary Christian Herter and his staff wanted to supply the Rusk group with all the information they needed and to bring them into discussions of pending policy problems, such as Laos, Berlin, and NATO armaments. At the same time the outgoing officials were aware of President Eisenhower's determination to retain full policy responsibility until Inauguration Day. They did not want to overstep limits set by the White House, which essentially discouraged the sharing of information below the Herter-Rusk level, but thought these limits too restrictive. In general, they resolved any uncertainties in the direction of cooperativeness and generosity, but felt the strain of discussing problems with officials who could not, as yet, do anything about them.

On the other hand, Secretary-designate Rusk and his associates were interested in getting information as rapidly as possible, yet reluctant (on instructions from the President-elect) to appear committed to policy decisions made by their predecessors. (One newcomer said he was afraid of being "brainwashed.")

Herter himself directed the preparation of voluminous briefing books covering both policy issues and information about organization and personnel, and personally reviewed these materials before they were turned over to the Rusk group. Material on administration was prepared by the office of the Deputy Under Secretary for Administration, Loy Henderson. This covered a wide spectrum of subjects, ranging from the duties and authority of the Secretary and the department's administrative philosophy to mail procedures and cafeteria locations. Substantive material on the various geographic areas was prepared by the bureaus concerned and was followed by a chapter on economic affairs.

Copies of the volume on substantive matters were labeled Top Secret and carefully controlled. Copies were given to Rusk, Bowles, George C. McGhee, who was to be Counselor and Chairman of the Policy Planning Council, and to W. Averell Harriman, who had been designated Ambassador-at-Large. Assistant Secretary-designate G. Mennen Williams and Adlai Stevenson, named Ambassador to the United Nations, were given an opportunity to read it. The administrative book went to fifteen of the top people in the new administration.

How much of the voluminous material was actually read and used to advantage is hard to say. It depended upon the official concerned—his work habits, how early he was appointed, how swamped he was with other concerns. In one curious lapse, a top administrative official did not learn until much later that the administrative briefing book existed. In general, Brookings interviews disclosed that the briefing materials were about right in scope and approach.

When Rusk arrived at the department the third week in December he was given a suite of offices on the ground floor and a staff. This included a special assistant, Emory C. Swank, a professional Foreign Service officer who had been deputy director of the department secretariat. Swank was to see that all materials received by Rusk came from Herter's office. This initial staff also included a secretary for Rusk, one for Swank, a security escort, and a telephone receptionist. Another Foreign Service officer joined the staff later in the month. Other new officials moved into the suite as their appointments were announced: Bowles, Williams, McGhee, and Ball.

During the month preceding inauguration Rusk and his associates were busy with the reports of the task forces, the department's briefing materials, and with innumerable appointments, telephone calls, and letters. They found the combination of task force reports and department briefing materials to be a good one: The former were political documents—conclusions without elaborate documentation. The latter provided copious information but no conclusions. Rusk was briefed daily by the Director of Intelligence and Research.

In general, Rusk became oriented quickly and smoothly, thanks to his previous experience and to Swank's help. The process seemed less satisfactory in the case of Bowles, who was less familiar with the department, and who had brought his own assistants with him. (He soon added a professional Foreign Service officer to his staff.) Members of both new and old teams thought a month too short a time to prepare a new group to take over such a complex establishment as the Department of State. Nevertheless, the new group had enough information and facilities at their disposal so that they were off to a fast start.

The "New Team" and Its Relationships

The new President had declared his intention of bringing more vigor, warmth, and clarity of purpose into the formulation and administration of American foreign policy. A crucial factor in achieving this aim would obviously be the effectiveness of the new leaders of the Department of State—their knowledge, their experience, and their ability to work with the President, the Congress, and with one another.

A good question at this point is, "How new were the members of the new team?" They were new in the responsibilities just assigned to them and new in their relationships to each other. Yet they were not strangers to the department, nor to problems of international relations. The 1961 group of presidential appointees was a mixture of former employees, career Foreign Service officers, and men whose previous work had brought them into contact with the department or with international matters. Such a mixture is the rule rather than the exception in the Department of State. The department never draws the sharp line between political officers and career staff that might be expected from elementary readings in American government (or from the "model" pattern outlined in Chapter 1).

The Presidential Appointees

As noted earlier, the new leadership of the department gave promise of outstanding performance, judging by previous experience. The extent to which this promise was fulfilled is most difficult to judge in such a dynamic field as the development and administration of foreign policy. Probably no norms of performance can be conceived except a mixture of incisiveness and thoroughness in advising the President and reasonable efficiency in carrying out his directions. Some judgments of quality can perhaps be based upon tenure, but this is a dangerous criterion in a bureaucracy. Others can be based upon the comments of the press, commentators, and experienced persons within the department.

THE SECRETARY. Secretary Rusk was obviously well prepared by experience for his responsibilities. His appointment was applauded by the Foreign Service professionals, who regarded him as a "semi-pro" in their field. He made clear from the outset his confidence in the career staff of the department, in contrast to the late Secretary John Foster Dulles, who had taken a critical, warning tone with them.[3] Rusk worked hard and rapidly to bring his own knowledge up to date. He was politic, yet frank, in his relations with Congress and the press. In general he gave the impression of being a competent, dedicated public servant and a warm human being.

The liking he inspired became mixed with sympathy as it soon became apparent that Rusk had to play two difficult roles. In one he served as head of a world-wide organization of some 24,000 employees performing the usual diplomatic, reporting, and service functions of the department. In the other role he served as one

[3] See partial text of Rusk's remarks to department employees in "The Essentials of our Foreign Policy," *Sunday Star* (Washington), March 12, 1961.

(and not the only) adviser on foreign policy to a vigorous President, whose denials that he was his own Secretary of State were less than totally convincing. For President Kennedy had placed such emphasis on foreign policy in his public statements and had such an intense interest in the subject that he was committed to a sort of personal management of the country's international relations.[4] Kennedy appointed McGeorge Bundy of Harvard University, a brilliant and thorough workman, as his Special Assistant on international security affairs, and Bundy acquired a staff. Assistant Secretaries of State were soon reporting a high degree of White House interest in their work, sometimes in the form of telephone calls from the President himself, sometimes in the form of questions or "second-guessing" by Bundy's staff. Another factor which helped push the management of foreign policy into the White House was the attitude of some of the President's confidants, who had little faith in the value of traditional diplomatic methods or in the effectiveness of the Department of State as an operating institution.[5]

Rusk was steadfastly cooperative (some critics said too patient) in this difficult situation. By 1963 members of his staff sensed increased White House confidence in the department, an increased tendency to treat the Secretary as a department head more than as a staff adviser. President Johnson, although he took an active part in diplomacy and in policy determination and although he retained Bundy, relied upon the Secretary's advice and treated him as head of a responsible and respected institution.

OTHERS IN THE TOP COMMAND. Although Under Secretary Bowles had served as Ambassador to India, he was not particularly familiar with the Washington work of the Department of State. He brought personal vigor and a fresh viewpoint to his job and

[4] This was clear a month before inauguration to the author of a Washington quip column: "Everything is working nicely at the State Department. Chester Bowles will be the Under Secretary, Dean Rusk the Secretary, and Jack Kennedy the oversecretary."—Fletcher Knebel, *Evening Star* (Washington), Dec. 16, 1960.

[5] Two reports by a close observer in 1962 reveal two of Kennedy's attitudes: (1) growing confidence in Rusk—E. W. Kenworthy, "Evolution of Our No. 1 Diplomat," *New York Times Magazine*, March 18, 1962, pp. 31, 136 ff.; and (2) his wish for more incisive performance by the department—Kenworthy, "President Prods His Policy Aides," *New York Times*, July 3, 1962.

worked hard and imaginatively at his initial major assignment, recommending ambassadorial candidates. It soon became clear, however, that his relationships were not satisfactory with the White House, with the Secretary, and with the career staff in general. His future in the job was shortened when he permitted word to get out that (although not consulted) he had been opposed to the ill-advised effort to support the invasion of Cuba by rebels. As early as July 1961 there were rumors of his departure, and in November he was "promoted" to Special Adviser to the President on African, Asian, and Latin American Affairs. In this capacity he was to represent the United States abroad—something Kennedy thought he did well.[6] Bowles was later named Ambassador to India—a position he had held with general approval at the end of the Truman administration.

After Bowles moved out of the Number Two job it was filled by Ball, who clearly enjoyed the confidence of Rusk and of Presidents Kennedy and Johnson. He was used as a top policy adviser and as a special envoy on difficult diplomatic problems, such as the Greco-Turkish hostilities in Cyprus and the proposal to establish a multilateral nuclear-armed NATO fleet. He devoted relatively little attention to the internal management of the department.

Other experienced members of the top command included:

George C. McGhee, an Assistant Secretary of State in the Truman administration, as Counselor and Chairman of the Policy Planning Council

W. Averell Harriman, former Ambassador to Great Britain, Governor of New York, and Secretary of Commerce, as Assistant Secretary for Far Eastern Affairs and later Under Secretary (Political)

Harlan Cleveland, editor, college dean, and former foreign aid official, as Assistant Secretary for International Organization Affairs

Edwin M. Martin, a career government economist and foreign service officer, as Assistant Secretary for Economic Affairs

[6] Chalmers M. Roberts, "Smoother-Running Foreign Policy Seen as Result of Shifts at State," *Washington Post*, Nov. 27, 1961.

Some of the members of Rusk's top staff, although well qualified by background and attitude, were not kept in their positions for prolonged periods. They apparently were not able to meet the numerous, difficult, and sometimes conflicting demands of the White House, the Congress, and the Foreign Service professionals. Philip H. Coombs, the Assistant Secretary for Educational and Cultural Affairs, although a well-known economist, educator, and former federal official, found it hard to adapt himself to the pressures of the job, particularly congressional relations. He resigned after a little more than a year in the job and was succeeded by Lucius D. Battle, who had been Executive Secretary of the department and had served in career posts in both the civil service and Foreign Service. Brooks Hays, the Assistant Secretary for Congressional Relations, also found it difficult to swim in the troubled waters of State-Congress relations despite his long service on Capitol Hill, and became an Assistant to the President after nine months.

Another short-termer was the Assistant Secretary for Public Affairs, Roger W. Tubby. In about a year it was announced that Tubby would represent the United States at the Geneva office of the United Nations. A newspaper story at that time mentioned the lack of close working relationship between Tubby and Rusk and Tubby's objections to restrictions on the release of certain diplomatic information and to budget limitations on his organization.[7] Chosen to succeed him was Robert J. Manning, another experienced journalist who had been bureau chief for *Time-Life* in London.

One of the more troublesome jobs from a personnel standpoint was one that perhaps most needed stable tenure—the top administrative job, Deputy Under Secretary for Administration. This position was held for the last five years of the Eisenhower administration by Loy W. Henderson, an experienced Foreign Service "pro." He was succeeded by Roger W. Jones, a long-time top official of the Bureau of the Budget, who had been for two years Chairman of the U. S. Civil Service Commission. Although Jones applied the administrative capacities that had won him honorary

[7] *Washington Post*, Jan. 28, 1962.

awards and public recognition, he became the victim of the White House general lack of confidence in the Department of State bureaucracy. Jones returned to the Bureau of the Budget in 1962 and was succeeded by William H. Orrick, a Department of Justice attorney closely associated with Robert Kennedy. Within a year Orrick too had "gone back where he came from"—Justice. The administrative leadership was then put in the hands of William J. Crockett, a veteran management specialist and Foreign Service officer. He was "backed up" by Dwight J. Porter, another "FSO" and experienced administrator, as Assistant Secretary for Administration.

REGIONAL ASSISTANT SECRETARIES AND AMBASSADORS. The five regional assistant secretaryships also showed variations in performance and stability. The stable ones—if any such jobs can be considered stable—were those concerned with Africa, Europe, and the Near East and South Asia. Governor Williams, whose appointment was the first announced for the department, "lit running" before the inauguration and kept his momentum. His combination of enthusiasm and inexperience caused worries in the Ball-Sharon task force group and later in the department, but many of the people of the new African nations came to regard him as a friend and advocate.

The Assistant Secretary for European Affairs was a highly regarded Foreign Service "pro," Foy D. Kohler, who had been appointed to the position by President Eisenhower late in 1959. Kohler was made Ambassador to the Soviet Union in August 1962 and was succeeded by another experienced career minister, William R. Tyler. Herter's Assistant Secretary for Near Eastern and South Asian Affairs, G. Lewis Jones, was kept on briefly, but then was sent to London in April 1961. He was succeeded by Phillips Talbot, a former newspaperman, political science professor and expert in Indian and Pakistani affairs.

The Far Eastern Bureau was headed by a succession of short-term assistant secretaries: Walter P. McConaughy, a career Foreign Service officer, for seven months, then Harriman for seventeen, Roger Hilsman for eleven, and finally William P. Bundy (brother of McGeorge), who had served as Assistant Secretary of Defense for International Security Affairs. Hilsman was reported to have resigned because he was bypassed in the department on Vietnamese matters.

Quick changes also characterized the post of Assistant Secretary for Inter-American Affairs. The new administration inherited Thomas C. Mann, a Texas lawyer who had become a career Foreign Service officer, but Mann was made Ambassador to Mexico in April 1961. The administration's difficulties in getting someone to take this job were commented upon in the press from time to time until July, when Robert F. Woodward, a career man, was appointed. A year later *he* was made an ambassador (Spain), and Edwin M. Martin, another Foreign Service officer, was chosen. All this time the Alliance for Progress was floundering, and political relationships between the United States and the Latin American countries had not improved and clarified to the degree hoped for at the start of the administration. President Johnson soon after his accession reappointed Mann as Assistant Secretary and began a number of personal diplomatic contacts with South-of-the-Border statesmen.

In the major ambassadorships, too, there were variations in tenure and qualifications, but the administration for the most part named career men and other citizens of first-rate qualifications.

THE PRESIDENTIAL APPOINTMENTS, IN SUMMARY. President Kennedy made an obvious and on the whole successful effort to make top quality appointments, selections of men with vigor and knowledge, for the administration of foreign policy. The effort was clouded, however, by a number of instances in which the appointees did not work out and were replaced. Several of these were handled as a group by Rusk personally. These were the Ball-for-Bowles, McGhee-to-Under Secretary (Political), Harriman-for-McConaughy, and Dutton-for-Hays changes in late 1961.

In part such shifts were needed because no executive ever "bats 1.000" in his initial selections. There are no reliable criteria for judging success in this field. The State Department's experience will be compared in later chapters with that of the other departments studied. Even these comparisons will mean little because of differences in personalities, political milieus, constituencies, the pressures of current events, and the closeness of relationships with the White House. The shifts also resulted from presidential and congressional pressures and from unanticipated operating conditions. Allowance must also be made for rotation in office due to the operations of the Foreign Service career system.

Even though mindful of these cautions and complexities, the observer must conclude that there was a great deal of change—more change than stability. Of the department's top team, only Rusk, Ball, Williams, Talbot, and Cleveland served throughout the Kennedy-Johnson term of four years. The other eleven top men who started out with Rusk (under secretaries, deputy under secretaries, and assistant secretaries) served an average (mean) of fourteen months in their positions. The median job tenure for all seventeen was seventeen months. This has to be judged an unstable situation, considering the complexity and importance of their responsibilities.

The Career Staff—Status and Morale

The Foreign Service professionals and the upper ranks of the civil service employees do the staff work to back up the presidential appointees. These career employees, regardless of the changes at top level, provide the work that holds the department together. The Foreign Service officers in particular represent the United States abroad, providing services to citizens, and reporting their observations. Some of these careerists, as we have seen, have risen to become ambassadors and assistant secretaries.

During the Eisenhower administration the "FSO's" tended to feel "left out" because Secretary Dulles conducted so much personal diplomacy and centralized decision-making in his own office. Morale had also been badly hurt by Senator Joseph McCarthy's attacks. Now the professionals welcomed Rusk's appointment, feeling that he would make fuller use of the Foreign Service.

The resulting lift in morale proved to be temporary, as the White House staff began dominating foreign policy work and conveying an impression of lack of confidence in the Department of State. The FSO's stock was on the rise again in 1963, and President Johnson in the early period of his presidency made clear his reliance on Secretary Rusk and his staff.

One top career official pointed out that dissatisfaction with the

Foreign Service is inevitable because of the sheer difficulty of the problems it works with and the lack of control the United States government has over many factors in international relations. The Foreign Service, then, may be looked to for good answers to questions for which there are no good answers.

THE HERTER COMMITTEE. Seeking to strengthen his career staff, Secretary Rusk requested a study of professional and executive personnel. The study was made in 1962 by a committee of distinguished citizens, headed by former Secretary Herter. Necessary resources were provided by foundations. Two of the key recommendations in the committee's report[8] never made any headway: appointment of a career Executive Under Secretary of State and establishment of a National Foreign Affairs College to provide postgraduate personnel training. Some progress has been made, however, on recommendations to establish career services in the Agency for International Development and the U.S. Information Agency and to strengthen recruitment activities. Officials acknowledge, however, that they have a long way to go in estimating needs for future manpower, in evaluating the abilities of personnel, in referring the best qualified persons for vacant jobs, and in general career management.

CAREERISTS IN THE TRANSITION. In general the career staff made positive contributions to the process of getting the new administration started. These consisted partly of their briefings, partly of the rich experience of those selected for top jobs, and partly of the day-to-day work of Foreign Service officers who continued to perform the same duties as they had under Secretary Herter, particularly at the deputy assistant secretary level.

Some Major Policy Developments in the Early Sixties

These "old hands" and newcomers, these careerists and noncareerists, were inevitably involved in foreign policy problems to which they could make only a partial contribution. The President

---

[8] *Personnel for the New Diplomacy: Report of the Committee on Foreign Affairs Personnel* (Carnegie Endowment for International Peace, December 1962).

must deal with such problems daily and in doing so he considers advice not only from the Secretary of State but from his own staff; from the Secretary of Defense; from the Directors of the Central Intelligence Agency, the Arms Control and Disarmament Agency, the U. S. Information Agency; from congressional leaders; and from many other sources. The Secretary of State provides access to the channels of diplomacy; he furnishes vital information from the missions abroad and from the department's staff and records; and he is certainly a primary adviser. Nevertheless, he cannot be given entire credit for successes nor full blame for errors in the nation's foreign policy.[9]

A resounding error occurred in the spring of 1961 when the United States encouraged yet did not adequately support an attempt by Cuban refugees to invade Cuba at the Bay of Pigs. President Kennedy took full responsibility for the mistake, but he had acted after being advised by State, as well as Defense and CIA officials. More effective evidences of firmness in confronting Communism were found in the President's refusal to back down in Berlin, his support of the United Nations peacekeeping mission in the Congo, and the increasing military support of South Vietnam. The confrontation became alarming—and successful—when the Cuban quarantine in the fall of 1962 resulted in the withdrawal of Soviet missiles from the island.

Some of the American policies resulted in strained relationships with our allies. There was British resentment, for example, when the United States canceled development of the Skybolt missile, expected to be an important weapon in Britain's deterrent force. Other strains resulted from France's threats to leave NATO and her opposition to American policies in South Vietnam. An American proposal for an international nuclear force had a controversial and inconclusive history.

A more successful Kennedy administration venture was the large-scale promotional and educational effort that led to the passage of the Trade Expansion Act of 1962. This law granted authority to the President for five years to enter into trade agree-

9 See, for example, Joseph Kraft's comments on Secretary Rusk's share in the foreign policies of the Kennedy and Johnson administrations in "The Enigma of Dean Rusk," *Harper's Magazine,* Vol. 231 (July 1965), pp. 100–03.

ments and to negotiate reductions of as much as 50 percent in American tariff rates.

In the latter months of the Kennedy administration relationships with the Soviet Union eased, and this period was highlighted by the signature of the nuclear test ban treaty in the autumn of 1963.

These events and many others were characteristic of a tense and dynamic state of international relations from 1961 to 1964 that kept the Department of State under constant pressure. The strain was increased by the accession of new world leaders: Brezhnev and Kosygin in Russia, Erhard in West Germany, Wilson in Great Britain, the new Pope, Paul VI, and President Johnson himself.

As State Department officials worked on these urgent problems in shifting patterns of relationships with the White House, the Pentagon, and other participants, it is not surprising that the personnel changes discussed above took place. There were organizational changes too, but perhaps fewer than might have been expected under the circumstances.

Organization: Better Focused Responsibility

Soon after President Kennedy took office he made clear his impatience with formalized interdepartmental coordinating machinery and with elaborate organization of the White House staff.[10] He generally preferred to hold one department head primarily responsible for a given policy area, including coordination of the work of other departments involved in that same area. This preference led within a month of the inauguration to the abolition of the Operations Coordinating Board, an interdepartmental group (with fifty subcommittees) established by President Eisenhower to follow up, in a coordinated way, on decisions of the National Security Council. Kennedy's executive order[11] was accompanied

[10] See, for example, Richard E. Neustadt, "Approaches to Staffing the Presidency: Notes on FDR and JFK," *American Political Science Review*, Vol. 57 (December 1963), pp. 861–63.

[11] No. 10,920, Feb. 18, 1961.

by a statement that responsibility for much of the board's work would be centered in the Secretary of State, with appropriate related functions being performed by the U. S. Information Agency and the White House staff.

This step was part of a general effort to strengthen the function of the department, to make it "the principal coordinating arm of the President in carrying out policies affecting our international relations." [12] To make this policy clear in the field, the President wrote to every ambassador on May 29, 1961, stressing his total responsibility for the United States Mission in his location, including supervision of representatives of other agencies there.

This focus of responsibility in the Department of State put fresh emphasis on the need for clear lines of supervision and communication *within* the department—a need to which an incoming executive would be attentive anyway. But Rusk was not able to start any organizational studies or changes before the Bay of Pigs episode tragically underlined the need for better machinery to assemble information at the right point and to evaluate proposed policies and actions. Meanwhile the President and his staff were demanding faster action by the department on their requests for information or for recommendations.

The Operations Center

An early step taken to meet these needs was the establishment of an "Operations Center" in the spring of 1961. This was a twenty-four-hour "command post" in the department where intelligence on current and potential crises could be sifted and evaluated by knowledgeable officials as fast as it came in. The center was also to be a headquarters from which the President could issue orders more speedily than if they were transmitted through normal diplomatic or intelligence facilities. A major proponent of the center was George McGhee, then Counselor of the department, and its director was Theodore C. Achilles, a long-time career Foreign Service officer and a former Counselor. Stephen Smith,

---

[12] Statement by Secretary Rusk before Senate Subcommittee on National Policy Machinery, Aug. 24, 1961, State Dept. Press Release No. 592.

the President's brother-in-law, served as unsalaried assistant to Achilles.

The center itself had an initial staff of only three. Each crisis was dealt with by a task force headed by the regional assistant secretary concerned, with help from the center staff and from personnel of other agencies, when appropriate. The task forces were to concentrate intensively on the problems reported and were to produce reports for the President. Task forces were established to work on such matters as the aftermath of the Cuban invasion, other Latin American difficulties, Vietnam, and colonial policy in Africa.

Proponents of the center pointed to its ability to give speedy, coordinated attention to particular problems by both State and non-State personnel; to its always-alert operation; and to its policy of reinforcing rather than weakening lines of responsibility within the department. The center also had symbolic and psychological impact: i.e., evidence that the Department of State was exercising leadership in the field of foreign policy.

Opponents expressed concern that the task forces would become autonomous of the responsible bureaus and would duplicate other twenty-four-hour watches. As time went on it was discovered that the center was no substitute for normal State Department operations or for interdepartmental coordination at the secretarial level. In January 1962 Smith resigned, and Achilles was reassigned, but the center continued to operate as a central twenty-four-hour alerting system and to serve task forces.

Other Organizational Changes

One organizational change made at the very beginning of the Kennedy administration was the upgrading of the educational and cultural affairs function—an activity which Kennedy had promised would receive more emphasis. The top job was made that of an assistant secretary (it had been a special assistant), and the Bureau of Educational and Cultural Affairs was organized along regional lines in order to facilitate expanded educational work with the developing nations.

Other changes followed a reexamination of the department's top structure. Late in 1961 Secretary Rusk appointed an expert six-man survey group headed by former Deputy Under Secretary Carlisle Humelsine.[13] Their report was never made public, but it led to further staff studies and to some new directives by the Secretary. The changes did not add up to a major shake-up or to a shift in fundamental organizational philosophy, but they did clarify responsibilities of top officials.

The Under Secretary, whose responsibility had not been clear, was made "full deputy and alter ego to the Secretary", and assigned to give "overall direction to the substantive functioning and day-to-day management of the department."[14] Under this directive Ball functioned as a chief of staff. There were frequent occasions, however, when his involvement in particular policy problems kept him from participation in the management of the department. The same directive also told the Under Secretary to guide foreign economic policy and international labor matters.

Probably the most significant change was that which made the Under Secretary for Political Affairs the top planner and coordinator of operational and political matters. Under the former organization he was only a staff adviser to the Secretary in coordinating foreign policy. The new directive placed him in charge of the geographic bureaus and the bureaus of International Organization Affairs, Educational and Cultural Affairs, and Intelligence and Research.

The directive also made it clear that the Deputy Under Secretary for Administration would continue to be in charge of the Bureaus of Administration and Security and Consular Affairs and the Foreign Service.

Thus the department was divided into two main parts, political and administrative, each reporting to a principal officer. Left out-

[13] Other members: William O. Hall and Walter K. Scott, both career foreign service officers and administrative specialists; Arthur Stevens, a former State Department administrative official; Robert Macy, Chief of the International Division of the Bureau of the Budget; and Ralph S. Roberts, who had been Administrative Assistant Secretary of Agriculture (see Chap. 5), now Deputy Assistant Secretary of State for Management.

[14] *Foreign Affairs Manual Circular No. 44*, Dec. 15, 1961.

side these two groups were a number of staff bureaus and offices, reporting to the Secretary and Under Secretary:

The Office of Congressional Relations

The Office of the Legal Adviser

The Bureau of Public Affairs

The Bureau of Economic Affairs

The Policy Planning Council—augmented and strengthened by the new administration

The Office of International Scientific Affairs—expanded from a small Office of Scientific Adviser (this office was given bureau status a year later)

The "Quasi-Independents"

The administration's emphasis on close-coupled foreign policy created an organizational dilemma for four agencies whose work seemed to call for some independence from the Department of State proper: those concerned with overseas information, disarmament, foreign aid, and volunteer service abroad. In all four instances organizational tidiness and the need for consistent policy argued for their incorporation in the Department of State. On the other hand, each agency had functions, relationships, and a history that set it apart from the mainstream of department functions. The problem was resolved in three different ways.

The United States Information Agency was left independent. Policy coordination was maintained through its Director's personal relationships with the Secretary, his attendance at meetings of the National Security Council, and staff consultations at lower levels, particularly with the Bureaus of Public Affairs, of Educational and Cultural Affairs, and Administration. The Director attended the Secretary's staff meetings and worked closely with the Deputy Under Secretary for Administration.

The Arms Control and Disarmament Agency, established in 1961, also remained an independent organization, but its Director was to serve as adviser to the Secretary of State as well as to the President. The agency appeared on the department's organization chart, attached to the Secretary and Under Secretary by that conveniently vague device, a dotted line. The Deputy Under Secretary of State for Political Affairs was assigned leadership and guidance responsibilities in this field, among others.

The third pattern was that followed by the Agency for International Development and the Peace Corps. Both were established within the Department of State by delegations of authority issued by the Secretary, but they functioned with considerable administrative independence. In the event of policy differences, however, there was no question that they were subject to the Secretary's authority.

Organization and Administration in General

There are abundant reasons why the Department of State will never compete for the honor of being the nation's (or the federal government's) most efficiently administered organization. Even more than in most federal departments, its plans and schedules are altered daily by current events or presidential decree, if not by congressional intervention. It cannot expect to be headed by a man greatly interested in internal efficiency. It must endlessly inform and consult with other departments. Its civil service administrative technicians must adapt themselves to the traditions and communications network of the Foreign Service. Coordination evolves more through a network of mutual consultation and clearance than through directives from above, and there are no absolute standards by which to judge achievements.

Granting all these difficulties, the Rusk regime at the department must be given credit for continuing efforts to achieve coherent organization and effective communication. Considering the department's mission, its political vulnerability, and its dual personnel system, stability among its key staff may be too much to hope for—however desirable.

The Budget: More Money; No More Jobs

Along with Rusk's emphasis upon clarity of organization went emphasis upon budgetary conservatism. He continually stressed, both within the department and on Capitol Hill, that the department must be "lean and fit." The budget did go up, of course—from about $307 million in fiscal year 1962 to $382 million for 1965.[15] The increases were for higher salaries and expenses (federal salaries were raised in 1962 and 1964), construction of buildings, contributions to international organizations, and greatly increased scope and volume of educational and cultural activities. During this period, however, the number of employees rose by only 1.5 percent. Much of this increase was in fiscal year 1965, when 131 communications jobs were added. Rusk was determined not to ask Congress for more jobs, and when new staffing needs arose (as they did in connection with the new African countries) they were met by squeezing other parts of the department.

The First Johnson Year

From the viewpoint of the Department of State staff, the change from Kennedy to Johnson was an easy one, apart from the sheer trauma of the assassination. Johnson assumed power confidently and smoothly and kept intact the White House staff concerned with foreign affairs. No policy changes were apparent. The major change was that the new President "meant business" on economy in staffing and administration. This was felt mainly in the form of manpower ceiling controls and later controls on upgrading civil service jobs. The President's general attitude seemed to be one of respect for the Secretary and confidence in the department, although as time went on he began to concern himself with more and more detailed matters of foreign policy.

Of three key State Department appointments made in the summer of 1964, one had a Johnsonian touch. Harry C. McPherson, Jr., a young (35) Texas lawyer who had spent five years on the staff of the Senate Democratic Policy Committee, was named Assistant Secretary for Educational and Cultural Affairs. His predecessor, Lucius Battle, was appointed Ambassador to the United Arab Republic. The third vacancy was filled by promotion. Assistant Secretary Manning (Public Affairs) resigned to

[15] Source: *The Budget of the United States Government.* Figure for 1962 is actual expenditure; for 1965, as enacted.

work for the *Atlantic Monthly* and was replaced by his deputy, James L. Greenfield, a former *Time-Life* correspondent. Early in 1965 Assistant Secretary Thomas Mann, also close to President Johnson, was promoted to Under Secretary for Economic Affairs.

A Smooth Transition

The Department of State in the early sixties was taken over competently and smoothly by a knowledgeable group: "old pros" and "semi-pros." They were well prepared by the work of the pre-inaugural task forces and by briefings within the department. Once started, some of them were found to be in the wrong spots, particularly in view of the dominant, high-pressure relationship of the White House to the department, and there were frequent changes in many of the key posts. Meanwhile organizational relationships were clarified and fiscal administration was kept conservative. The professional Foreign Service continued to perform competently and produced able candidates for assistant secretaryships and ambassadorships.

The government's total organization for developing and administering foreign policy was in its typical (and perhaps inevitable) condition of stress and turmoil, a condition that would have been worse if the State Department take-over had not been well managed.

3 / THE DEPARTMENT OF DEFENSE
A New Way of Doing Business

> . . . I have, therefore, instructed the Secretary of Defense
> to reappraise our entire defense strategy: our ability to fulfill
> our commitments; the effectiveness, vulnerability and dis-
> persal of our strategic bases, forces, and warning systems;
> the efficiency and economy of our operation and organiza-
> tion; the elimination of obsolete bases and installations;
> and the adequacy, modernization, and mobility of our pres-
> ent conventional and nuclear forces and weapons systems
> in the light of present and future dangers.
>
> —President Kennedy
> State of the Union Message,
> January 29, 1961

WHILE THE "OLD HANDS" at State
were making a brisk start in 1961, a new group at Defense seemed
even brisker. And while much of the motive power and control
of foreign policy came from the White House, the new push at
the Department of Defense came from its Secretary.

Robert S. McNamara, then aged 45, had been president of the
Ford Motor Company for hardly a month when he was designated by President-elect Kennedy as Secretary of Defense. Mc-
Namara's background as a professor of business administration
and industrial comptroller led naturally to the analytical, cost-
conscious, incisive approach that characterized his administration.
This approach, aided by an unusual capacity for work and a willingness to make politically and bureaucratically unpopular decisions, resulted in startling changes in the management of half of

the federal government: the Department of Defense. McNamara could not have made these changes without resolute and understanding presidential support, but the skills and energy needed came from the Secretary and his staff. Nor could he have made them without the increased authority given the Secretary by the Department of Defense Reorganization Act of 1958.[1]

The Running Start

Kennedy announced his choice of McNamara in mid-December 1960. Within a few days the Secretary-designate had established headquarters in a Washington hotel and was busy recruiting staff, absorbing information, and planning. Various prominent citizens were asked to suggest candidates, and the "talent hunters" were consulted. He was able to put together a team of assistants who combined freshness of viewpoint with pertinent experience. Well before Inauguration Day McNamara was holding staff meetings and making assignments to these people.

In terms of policy objectives, McNamara's assignment was clear —and crushing. The President had directed him to take a fresh look at everything and make it better. Deterrent strength, invulnerability, versatility, efficiency, and economy were all to be achieved. Behind this assignment lay Kennedy's campaign declarations and a Democratic platform that called for:

1. Deterrent military power such that the Soviet and Chinese leaders will have no doubt that an attack on the United States would surely be followed by their own destruction.
2. Balanced conventional military forces which will permit a response graded to the intensity of any threats of aggressive force.
3. Continuous modernization of these forces through intensified research and development, including essential programs now slowed down, terminated, suspended, or neglected for lack of budgetary support.

A first order of business of a Democratic administration will be a complete reexamination of the organization of our armed forces.

[1] 72 Stat. 514. See particularly secs. 2 and 3.

A military organization structure, conceived before the revolution in weapons technology, cannot be suitable for the strategic deterrent, continental defense, limited war, and military alliance requirements of the 1960's.

We believe that our armed forces should be organized more nearly on the basis of function, not only to produce greater military strength, but also to eliminate duplication and save substantial sums.[2]

Advance planning also had to take account of the findings of two pre-inauguration task force reports. One on "National Security", prepared by a group headed by Paul H. Nitze, later to become Assistant Secretary of Defense for International Security Affairs and subsequently Secretary of the Navy, was never made public. Another, on organization of the national defense establishment, was the work of a committee chaired by Senator Stuart Symington, former Secretary of the Air Force. This report stirred up considerable controversy (see the discussion of organization later in this chapter). Roswell L. Gilpatric, a Truman administration veteran who became McNamara's deputy, was a member of both task forces.

Help in Getting Started

At the Pentagon, as at the State Department, the new team had ample help from its predecessors and from the career staff in getting started. The usual proclivity of the military for briefings and thorough staff work would have resulted in careful planning for the transition in any event. All three types of players in the drama —Eisenhower appointees, Kennedy appointees, and the career staffs, both military and civilian—took their cues from the Eisenhower-Kennedy talks, and the process acquired warmth and emphasis. McNamara and the outgoing Secretary, Thomas S. Gates, Jr., established a good working relationship immediately. Virtually all persons interviewed by Brookings staff reported attitudes of businesslike cooperation, although some mentioned the natural wariness of the new team to accept information and views from the career staff. In most cases the volume of written briefing

[2] "Complete Text of 1960 Democratic Platform," *Congressional Quarterly Weekly Report,* Vol. 18 (July 15, 1960), p. 1236.

materials was too much for the absorptive powers of the new-comers, considering the work pressures and the time available, but they knew the material was there for reference. Oral briefings were carefully planned and given.

The familiarization was aided further by installing newcomers in offices near their predecessors. McNamara, for example, moved in near Gates on January 2. Nitze was given an office near John Irwin, Assistant Secretary for International Security Affairs; Charles Hitch, designee for Assistant Secretary (Comptroller) became a tenant of Assistant Secretary Franklin B. Lincoln, Jr.; and General Counsel Vincent Burke made room for Cyrus Vance, his successor-to-be.

In the military departments there was the same positive, thorough approach to the take-over as in the Office of the Secretary of Defense: well-planned briefings, voluminous material on department organization and programs, and move-in-early cooperation. In the Navy, for example, a nine-page briefing list covered fourteen major topics on mission, administration, and current problems. The Army gave its new appointees a 150-page book on its philosophy, organization, and activities; a booklet of personnel information for presidential appointees (travel, benefits, conflict of interest rules, etc.); a 3½ inch book full of directives and statutory references; a booklet summarizing the backgrounds of key personnel; a summary of current major problems—including priority decisions facing the new Secretary; a history of the Army from 1955 to 1961, written by professional historians; and a set of organization charts. Equally impressive examples could have been chosen from the Air Force. And throughout the department the newcomers overcame their initial wonderment that the word "briefing" could be associated with such volumes of material. In general there was agreement that the process of handing over information and advice had been managed with thoroughness, goodwill, and dispatch.

Returnees, Holdovers, Late Arrivals

The running start was made easier by the fact that some of the appointees had previous experience in the department. Heading this list was Deputy Secretary of Defense Roswell L. Gilpatric, who had been Under Secretary of the Air Force in 1953. Also prominent among these returnees was the new Air Force Secretary, Eugene Zuckert, who had been Assistant Secretary of the Air Force under President Truman, and then a member of the Atomic Energy Commission. There was also Thomas D. Morris, a former Deputy Assistant Secretary of Defense for Installations and Logistics, now named Assistant Secretary. Another was William Schaub, former top man on military budgets at the Bureau of the Budget, who was now Assistant Secretary of the Army for Financial Management.

The transition was speeded up and made easier by the fact that some Eisenhower appointees remained for several months in the new administration. Several of these were "R&D types": Herbert York, Director, and John H. Rubel, Deputy Director of Research and Engineering; James H. Wakelin, Jr., Assistant Secretary of the Navy for Research and Development; and Joseph V. Charyk, Under Secretary of the Air Force. The Air Force also kept on its top legal and finance officials, Max Golden, General Counsel, and Lyle S. Garlock, Assistant Secretary for Financial Management.

A counterbalancing factor was the slowdown caused by some late appointments, resulting from problems in finding candidates, persuading them to take the jobs, or clearing them. A few examples can be given, without identifying any of these factors with any individual: Elvis Stahr, Secretary of the Army; Paul Fay, Under Secretary of the Navy; Joseph Imirie, Assistant Secretary (Materiel), and Brockway McMillan, Assistant Secretary (Research and Development) of the Air Force.

The Analytical Approach:
Programming, Budget, and Procurement

It was clear from the beginning that McNamara intended to use the Secretary's statutory powers to *manage* the Department of Defense in a more analytical, controlled, decisive, and detailed manner than it had ever been managed before. This was a change more in the department's way of doing business than in its organization structure, although organization was also examined intensively.[3] It was a change inextricably mingled with the experience, viewpoints, and work capacities of the Secretary's team.

Hitch and the "Package" Program

Most participants in the DOD changeover agree that the most important element in the new way of doing business was what was popularly called "program package budgeting"—a loose and too-narrow term. Better labels were the general "Programming System for the Office of the Secretary of Defense" and the more specific "Five Year Force Structure and Financial Program." The new approach to the enormous problems of planning and pricing military programs was primarily the work of Charles J. Hitch, a 51-year-old RAND Corporation economist and former Oxford tutor, chosen by McNamara to be Assistant Secretary of Defense (Comptroller). Hitch was the principal author of a 1960 book which explained how techniques of economic analysis could be applied to military problems.[4] This approach was consistent with McNamara's own views and seemed to fit the need for the reappraisal directed by the President.

Hitch was temporarily delayed in putting his views into practice because he was thrown into urgent activity to amend the fiscal 1962 budget proposed by former President Eisenhower. The principal amendments were designed to "strengthen and protect our strategic deterrent" (more Polaris submarines, more SAC bombers on ground alert, expanded space research) and to "strengthen and make more versatile our limited war deterrent" (expansion of airlift capability, increased development and procurement of nonnuclear weapons and equipment).[5]

Even so he was able to develop the outlines of the new budget policy, get it approved by the Secretary in May 1961, and announce it in testimony before the Senate Subcommittee on Na-

[3] See the next major section of this chapter.

[4] Charles J. Hitch and Roland N. McKean, *The Economics of Defense in the Nuclear Age* (Harvard University Press, 1960).

[5] *Department of Defense Appropriations for 1962*, Hearings before a Subcommittee of the House Appropriations Committee, 87 Cong. 1 sess. (1961), Pt. 3, pp. 5–6.

tional Policy Machinery on July 24.[6] Grappling with a problem he later described as "the maximization of our military capabilities through the rational allocation of available resources,"[7] Hitch proposed developing cost estimates, over a five-year period, for military resources, grouped by function, rather than by service. As the system was developed, there were ten major military programs, such as Strategic Retaliatory Forces, Continental Air and Missile Defense Forces, and General Purpose Forces. Each major program was divided into subaggregations. "These in turn are made up of 'program elements' which we consider the basic building blocks as well as the decision-making level of the programming process."[8] Examples of such program elements were the B-52 bomber force, armored Army divisions, and anti-submarine warfare aircraft carriers. Program elements were measured in physical terms wherever possible, and their full costs were estimated year by year and projected at least five years into the future.

This program planning and budgeting structure made it possible for the Secretary of Defense and the President to decide upon the size and makeup of military forces in terms of major policy objectives and on the basis of studies showing the relative effectiveness and costs of various force structures and weapons systems. There were also provisions for timely progress reporting and for continuous appraisal of programs so that necessary changes could be made as different needs developed or as improved approaches became available.[9]

The new system stressed decisions on allocation of resources, thus bypassing formal organizational lines which had handicapped previous Secretaries in making program decisions. This was a major change from the Eisenhower administration practice of imposing dollar ceilings on each of the military departments,

---

[6] New York Times, July 25, 1961.

[7] "Remarks of Assistant Secretary of Defense Charles J. Hitch at the Tenth Annual Meeting of the Western Section, Operations Research Society of America, Honolulu, Hawaii, September 14, 1964" (process), p. 1.

[8] Ibid., p. 3.

[9] The Defense programming and budgeting system is also summarized in Study Report on the Programming System for the Office of the Secretary of Defense, Department of Defense, June 25, 1962 (1963); and in Hitch's statement before the Military Operations Subcommittee of the House Government Operations Committee, July 25, 1962.

which then had to curtail some programs if they wanted to expand others.

Hitch had originally planned to put the system into effect over an eighteen-month period, during which trial runs would be made of about half a dozen well-defined programs. McNamara wanted faster progress, however, believing that if the system were not installed early, it would not be installed at all. He ordered that the new plan be put into effect in preparing the fiscal 1963 budget. This meant immediate action (and near-panic conditions throughout the military departments) in the summer of 1961.[10]

THE PLAN'S RECEPTION. The military bureaucracy responded cooperatively and vigorously, and the system was installed in that year, although considerable later patching was required. One cynical participant said that the military simply weren't organized to resist McNamara's innovations. A kinder and more prevailing judgment was that military officers are trained to respond to leadership and that the new system was simply a further application of analytical methods they were already using. There were (and still are) criticisms that computers were replacing seasoned military judgments. The answer was that military judgments *were* being considered, and in fact had more opportunity to influence decisions than in the past. Acceptance of the programming system grew steadily over the next three years, and military department officials who had been lukewarm at first became enthusiastic. Everyone concerned realized that the net effect of the new system was to move into the Office of the Secretary of Defense many types of decisions previously made by (or below) the military department secretaries.

STRATEGIC AND COST EFFECTIVENESS STUDIES. The "program package" system provided a background and framework for detailed studies of the effectiveness of various military approaches in terms of their technical merit and economic costs. Secretary McNamara insisted on evaluation of alternative solutions for broad strategy problems and on cost effectiveness studies of proposed weapons systems.[11] Beginning early in 1961 he ordered hundreds of stud-

[10] "Remarks of Assistant Secretary of Defense Charles J. Hitch," *op. cit.*, p. 5.
[11] "How the Budget Decisions Are Reached," *Armed Forces Management,* Vol. 9 (April 1963), p. 13.

ies, some large, some small; some done by OSD staff, some by individual military departments, some by interdepartmental task forces, some by nonprofit research organizations (RAND, Research Analysis Corporation, the Center of Naval Analyses, the Institute of Defense Analyses) or by other contractors. Over 100 studies had been ordered by March 1961 in a series of secretarial directives known as "McNamara's trombones," covering topics ranging from the use of atomic weapons in wartime to preparation of a glossary of military terms.[12] To help monitor the studies and bring the results together Hitch appointed one of his RAND associates, Alain C. Enthoven, as Deputy Assistant Secretary for Systems Analysis.[13]

Morris: Installations, Logistics, Cost Reduction

Another analytical way of doing business was promoted by the staff of the Assistant Secretary for Installations and Logistics. Thomas D. Morris, who moved into that position after a few months as Assistant Director of the Bureau of the Budget, was a forty-eight-year-old organization and systems expert who had divided his career among government, industry, and management consulting. He was in a new job combining the work of two previous assistant secretaries: one for Supply and Logistics, the other for Properties and Installations. The need for such a merger had been recognized (and recommended) before the Kennedy administration. The combination was a matter of apprehension on Capitol Hill because the two offices worked with different and

[12] *Washington Post,* March 25, 1961.

[13] Like any important development, the emphasis on military cost effectiveness studies generated spoofs. One contemplated the application of such studies to a service baseball team. Sample dialogue:

GENERAL BATT: Well, you see, sir, in baseball one of the players is called the "pitcher." He throws the ball very hard at the catcher, and the ball might be a fast ball, a slow ball, a curve ball, a slider, a sinker, or a knuckle ball.

MR. B. (a cost study expert): Well, I think right here we can cut down on the number of different kinds of balls. . . .

GENERAL BATT: Sir, it's the same ball, just thrown differently.

Frank Walker, "Who's On First?" *Armed Forces Management,* Vol. 10 (September 1964), p. 71.

very interested Senate subcommittees. Secretary McNamara had to do some personal missionary work with the senators concerned before he went ahead with the change.

The unified office acted for the Secretary in matters concerned with property, procurement, and supply—taking leadership on Defense-wide policies and doing staff work on matters requiring action by the Secretary. (Each of the military departments provided logistical support for its own forces.)

Morris spearheaded McNamara's "Cost Reduction Program," a concentrated continuing effort to improve operating efficiency and reduce costs. This program ranks with the "program package" plan as a major management advance of the McNamara administration. Impressive progress was made in the 1962 and 1963 fiscal years—there were reported savings of $1.4 billion in 1963. The program acquired special meaning and emphasis when President Johnson took office. When the lights went off in the White House,[14] they stayed on in federal departments and agencies as officials worked on ways of keeping costs down.

The Defense Cost Reduction Program, which found savings of $2.8 billion in fiscal year 1964 and aimed at $4.8 billion in 1968 and each following year,[15] was more than an effort to make existing procedures more efficient. It raised basic questions about existing equipment and practices and initiated studies to find the answers—all without reducing military strength and combat readiness. The main elements of the program were simply stated:

1. Buying only what we need:
   a. Refining requirements calculations. *Example:* Reducing by $160 million requirements for air-to-air and air-to-ground missiles.
   b. Increased use of excess inventories. *Example:* Use by the Marine Corps of excess Army 120 mm. shells.
   c. Eliminating "goldplating" (unnecessary qualitative

---

[14] A widely and jocularly publicized symbol of the President's determination to achieve economies.

[15] These figures and the program description that follows are from a brochure, *Department of Defense Cost Reduction Program* (verbatim reprint of Secretary McNamara's Second Annual Progress Report to the President dated 7 July 1964).

features). *Example:* Substituting a commercial-type truck transmission for a specially designed, more costly military transmission.

2. Buying at the lowest sound price:

a. Shifting from non-competitive to competitive price procurement. Competitive price bidding was used for a steadily increasing percentage of contract awards—39.1 percent in 1964, up from 32.9 percent in 1961.

b. Shifting from cost-plus to fixed-price contracts—reducing the former from 38 percent in 1961 to 12 percent in 1964. Other contracts were written to include profit incentive formulas. The principal contractor for the TITAN III Space Booster, for example, could increase his fee from $6 million to $35 million (2¼ to 12¼ percent) depending on how well he met performance, schedule, and cost goals.

[Meanwhile one of Morris's colleagues, Harold Brown, Director of Defense Research and Engineering, launched a Contractor Performance Evaluation Program to aid in future selection of "R&D" contractors on the basis of their previous performance on Defense contracts.]

3. Reducing operating costs:

a. Terminating unnecessary operations, i.e., reducing or closing military installations—126 such actions in 1964, saving $252 million. The department usually phases these reductions over a period of several years to cushion the blow. Its Office of Economic Adjustment works with the communities affected to develop "a stronger and more permanent economic base than that which they had when they were heavily dependent upon military spending. Furthermore we are guaranteeing new job opportunities for civilian career employees who are displaced by base closings . . ."[16]

[This aspect of cost reduction took on new emphasis under President Johnson, who permitted McNamara to damn the political torpedoes and announce the closing of ninety-five additional bases including such historic facil-

---

[16] *Ibid.,* p. 16.

ities as the Brooklyn Navy Yard and the Springfield (Massachusetts) Armory.]

b. Consolidation and standardization of operations. This was merger of support operations previously handled separately by the military departments, notably through creation of the Defense Supply Agency in January 1962. DSA integrated the management of 1.6 million common supply items. Savings in 1964 were $42 million.

c. Increasing operating efficiency and economies in other support functions, such as communication systems, traffic management, and maintenance management.

The Cost Reduction Program was given publicity both within and outside the Department of Defense, climaxed by a "Cost Reduction Week" Pentagon ceremony at which the President commended the entire effort and presented awards to military officers and civilian employees for outstanding economy achievements.

No management-wise observer of, or participant in, the Cost Reduction Program would claim that its concepts or techniques were innovations. The new elements were the intensity of the effort and the top organizational level at which it was stimulated and recognized.

Brown: "R&D"

Interwoven with the budgeting-planning program and the Cost Reduction Program was a third phase of controlled, analytical management: the administration of research, development, test, and evaluation programs. The Department of Defense Reorganization Act of 1958 had set up the job of Director of Defense Research and Engineering and given the Director precedence over every official of the department except the Secretary, Deputy Secretary, and the military department secretaries.[17] The Director was made the Secretary's "principal adviser on scientific and technical matters," given supervision over "all research and engineering activities in the Department of Defense," and authorized to "*direct and control* . . . research and engineering activities that

[17] 72 Stat. 520, Sec. 9.

the Secretary of Defense deems to require centralized management."[18]

Under this authority Harold Brown, the new Director of Defense Research and Engineering, a young (34) Columbia-trained physicist recruited from the University of California's Radiation Laboratory, began subjecting the military department's research and development projects to an unprecedented degree of scrutiny and control. He and his staff had the power (and used it) to change details of R&D projects in the Army, Navy, and Air Force.

One of Brown's principal methods was the "project definition study." This was a painstaking review of any "R&D" program made after it had moved through research, "exploratory development," and "advanced development" and before it moved into "engineering development." Such a study

> . . . establishes for the Department and for the contractor exactly what is wanted, how it is to be designed and built, what it should cost, and how the program is to be managed. Thus, assurance is provided before large resources are committed that the performance, cost, and time factors are chosen to yield greatest military usefulness and that the preliminary research has provided all the essential elements for full-scale development. Moreover, this approach permits the establishment of firm goals and time schedules and reduces the chances for substantial cost overruns which have traditionally occurred in these stages of development.[19]

Effect on Overall Budget and Civilian Staffing

The management programs and controls described above were intended to achieve the greatest possible effectiveness for each dollar spent, or for each employee hired. Gross budget and staffing figures, therefore, do not tell much of the story, but it may be of interest to examine the figures for fiscal years 1961 through 1966 given in the table that follows,[20] which show that expenditures

---

[18] *Ibid.* Italics supplied.

[19] *Department of Defense Annual Report for Fiscal Year 1963,* p. 37.

[20] Source: *The Budget of the United States Government* for the fiscal years concerned. Figures for military functions include military assistance.

rose slightly and civilian employment fell during the period. Note the braking effect of the Johnson presidency in 1964 and 1965, a phenomenon also visible in the other departments studied.

Fiscal Year	Actual Expenditures (in millions)		Actual Employment	
	Military Functions	Civil Functions	Military Functions	Civil Functions
1961	$44,676	$ 972	1,012,375	30,032
1962	46,815	999	1,038,132	31,411
1963	49,973	1,128	1,017,117	32,648
1964	49,760	1,153	997,863	31,893
1965 (enacted)	47,875	1,265	980,000	31,990
1966 (est.)	47,900	1,337	961,000	32,500

The Organization Behind the Management

The new management made more of a change in the department's ways of doing business than in its formal organization structure. Nevertheless, organization was analyzed intensively and important changes were made.

Leadership in this effort was provided by a group led by lawyers, staffed by military officers, and innocent of "professional" organization and management experts. (The fact that the group's analytical powers were equal to the need should stimulate sober reflection and possible research by management societies.)

When McNamara came to the department he was "horrified," according to one assistant secretary, to find no top staff responsible for organization studies. He asked Cyrus Vance, his General Counsel, to take on this responsibility, and Vance devoted about half his time to this work in the early months of the new administration. Vance at forty-four was a New York lawyer who had been counsel to two Senate committees concerned with military matters. Working leadership was provided by Solis Horwitz, a Pittsburgh attorney with considerable federal experience in both the legislative and executive branches. Horwitz was aided by a staff of officers from all the services. This group served McNamara not only as his top "O & M" staff but as special troubleshooters. (They spent many hours on the TFX airplane investigation.)

The Symington Report

Even before Inauguration Day McNamara and his advisers were confronted with fundamental issues of department organization which became public and controversial. President-elect Kennedy's "Committee on the Defense Establishment," headed by Senator Symington,[21] proposed abolishing the offices of the secretaries of the military departments. The committee's report recommended that the military departments continue to give the armed forces administrative and logistic support but under their respective chiefs of staff; thus one layer of civilian control would be eliminated. The report also proposed: (1) replacement of the assistant secretaries of Defense by two under secretaries, one for administration and one for weapons systems; (2) reorganization of the Joint Chiefs of Staff to de-emphasize members' identification with their respective services; (3) creation of three unified commands (Strategic, Tactical, and Continental Defense) and specified area commands; and other changes. The major purpose was to strengthen the Secretary's ability to act "with unquestioned authority and control over *all elements* of the Department of Defense at *all levels.*"[22]

McNamara, emerging from a conference on December 20, 1960, with Representative Carl Vinson, Chairman of the House Armed Services Committee, told the press he would move slowly on reorganization matters.[23] The Symington Report was soon publicly attacked by Congressman Vinson and by the Chief of Naval Operations, Admiral Arleigh Burke. McNamara never directly confronted the issue of the military departments' organizational in-

---

[21] Other members (all lawyers): Clark M. Clifford, Kennedy's transition liaison man; Thomas K. Finletter, former Secretary of the Air Force, and his former Under Secretary, Roswell L. Gilpatric, soon to become Deputy Secretary of Defense; Fowler Hamilton, later to be Administrator of the Agency for International Development; and Marx Leva, former General Counsel of the DOD.

[22] *Report to Senator Kennedy from Committee on the Defense Establishment,* Dec. 5, 1960 (process), p. 9.

[23] *Washington Post,* Dec. 21, 1960.

tegrity but proceeded with the minimum changes in structure that seemed necessary to make his control effective.

Changes in OSD, JCS, and the DOD Agencies

OSD. In the Office of the Secretary of Defense a couple of changes reduced the number of assistant secretaries and brought together functions with some interests in common. One was the combination of Supply and Logistics with Properties and Installations, already mentioned. The other put the health and medical affairs function under Manpower. A new assistant secretary job was created to give more emphasis and visibility to the civil defense function, which the new President had moved to the Department of Defense. (Three years later this was reassigned to the Department of the Army.)

Several of the assistant secretaries, finding themselves without enough hands to keep up with the volume and pressure of the McNamara style of operation, added deputies or directors to their staffs. Examples: Hitch's Deputy for Systems Analysis; Morris's Director of Economic Adjustment; a Deputy for International Logistics Negotiations in the Office of the Assistant Secretary for International Security Affairs; a Deputy for Security Policy in the Office of the Assistant Secretary for Manpower; and two new deputies under the Director of Defense Research and Engineering.

A job of Assistant Secretary for Administration, a commonplace in other departments, was not created until 1964. Meanwhile Horwitz was working on organization, and OSD administrative services were managed by J. Robert Loftis, a long-service career man. Loftis's job was abolished after an audit disclosed fiscal irregularities. His duties, after an interval in which they were distributed between Hitch and Norman Paul (Assistant Secretary for Manpower) were finally put under Horwitz, who became Assistant Secretary for Administration. This new office included Horwitz's previous organizational study duties and a newly created Office of Inspection Services, a top "I.G." for the Secretary. Horwitz was also to serve as McNamara's assistant on matters involving the National Communications System, a worldwide interdepartmental network of "long-haul" communications facilities.

JCS AND THE COMMANDS.[24] Organization study of the Joint Chiefs of Staff resulted in comparatively little change in basic structure. In the Joint Staff, the Plans and Programs group ("J-5") was strengthened to reflect the increased activity of JCS in programming and budget formulation work. Its Intelligence Coordinating group ("J-2") was abolished and its functions given to the Defense Intelligence Agency (see below). Four new organizations were set up to meet supervisory, planning, and training needs: the National Military Command Center, the Joint Command and Control Requirements Group, the Joint War Games Agency, and the Defense Intelligence School.

At the command level units of the Strategic Army Corps and the Tactical Air Command were made into the new U. S. Strike Command in 1962. This was to serve as a reserve for the combat-ready commands already in existence. In 1963 "Stricom" was given responsibility for the Mideast, South Asia, and Africa south of the Sahara. Creation of the Strike Command resulted in assignment of almost all combat-ready forces to the unified and specified commands. Other organizational adjustments were made in the commands to increase the authority of their commanders-in-chief over subordinate military elements.

DOD AGENCIES. Two new major agencies outside the military departments were established in 1961.[25] The Defense Intelligence Agency, set up in August, absorbed and coordinated the headquarters intelligence work previously done by the military departments.

---

[24] It is useful to keep in mind the official statement of DOD command relationships:

"Commanders of unified and specified commands are responsible to the President and the Secretary of Defense for the accomplishment of military missions assigned to them. The chain of command runs from the President to the Secretary of Defense and through the Joint Chiefs of Staff to the commanders of unified and specified commands. Orders to such commanders are issued by the President or the Secretary of Defense, or by the Joint Chiefs of Staff by authority and direction of the Secretary of Defense. These commanders have full operational control over the forces assigned to them and perform such missions as are assigned by the Secretary of Defense with the approval of the President."

United States Government Organization Manual 1964-65, pp. 131–32.

[25] Two others, the Defense Atomic Support Agency (1959—formerly the Armed Forces Special Weapons Project) and the Defense Communications Agency (1960) were already in business.

The Defense Supply Agency was established in November 1961 to manage the supplying of items needed in common by the services. Steps had been taken in this direction long before the Kennedy administration through the "single manager" system under which one military department procured certain classes of items for all. Navy, for example, supplied medical items and petroleum; Army, food and clothing. This arrangement, although better than having each service do all its own buying, still was not satisfactory to the military consumer because of variations in forms and procedures. The DSA took over six existing and four planned "single manager" assignments and a variety of other functions related to procurement and supply, such as the Defense Materiel Utilization Program, the Federal Catalog program, and the Defense Scientific and Technical Documentation Services. By the end of fiscal year 1964 McNamara and Morris reported that DSA had achieved a 20 percent reduction in the personnel previously needed to do its work, and a 20 percent reduction in inventories. One reason that DSA got off to a good start was that McNamara told the military services informally but emphatically that they were to assign first-rate talent to the new organization.

Further unification of procurement-related work continued with the establishment of the Defense Contract Audit Agency, supplanting military department audit groups, and of Defense-wide Contract Administration Services[26] to handle security checks, acceptance checks, and all the other detailed work of contract administration. The former reports to the Secretary; the latter is part of DSA.

The three military departments continued to be assigned functions of joint interest. Army, for example, was given language training to manage; Navy, computer training; and Air Force, air intelligence training. Army, as already noted, was also given the civil defense responsibility.

Changes in the Military Departments

Within the Army, Navy, and Air Force there were important organizational changes designed to focus responsibility for planning and project administration and to ease communication with

[26] Being planned at this writing.

the Office of the Secretary of Defense. One change, ordered by McNamara, standardized the functions of the under secretaries and assistant secretaries of the military departments, who previously had been assigned varying combinations of duties. Under the new scheme each military department had one assistant secretary for financial management, one for research and development, and one for installations and logistics. Thus each one had an "opposite number" in the other services and in OSD, and communication was made easier. The under secretaries were intended to be general deputies, but their actual duties varied with their own experience and capacities.

There were also changes in major components of the services made after large-scale organization studies.

ARMY. In January 1962 Secretary of the Army Elvis Stahr announced a major reorganization of the Army, planned after a study made by some sixty officers and civilians. The main feature of the plan was the creation of a new Army Materiel Command to assume the job of developing, producing, and testing materiel—previously done by the "tech services," such as Ordnance, Signal, and Quartermaster. The new command took over direction of the technical services' field installations. The change caused some grumbling among officers, but no major controversy, and the net result seemed to be well-coordinated progress.[27] The new organization was consistent with the analytical, project-oriented approach of the Office of the Secretary of Defense.

The same organization study resulted in establishment of a new Combat Developments Command, responsible for new doctrine, preparation of field manuals and tables of organization, and for war games. At the same time most military training functions were assigned to the Continental Army Command, and military personnel assignment work was centralized in a new Office of Personnel Operations.

NAVY. About a year after the Army announcement the Navy announced a reorganization too. This stemmed from the Report of

27 See "One Year After the Shake-Up," *Armed Forces Management,* Vol. 9 (August 1963), pp. 18–20; and C. W. Borklund, "Has Army Materiel Command Earned Its Fourth Star?" *Armed Forces Management,* Vol. 10 (September 1964), pp. 36–38.

an Advisory Committee on the Review of the Management of the Department of the Navy, headed by John H. Dillon, Administrative Assistant to the Secretary. The rest of the committee consisted of two admirals, a Marine general, and a management consultant. The report contained eighty-five recommendations covering the total scope of Navy management. Principal changes were:

1. Revision of planning, programming, and budgeting systems into an integrated operation consistent with the OSD approach. A vice admiral in charge of program planning was placed in the office of the Chief of Naval Operations. Navy-wide project management systems were decreed.

2. Creation of "a single producer executive"—a Chief of Naval Materiel, in charge of the Bureaus of Weapons, Ships, Supplies and Accounts, and Yards and Docks. The objective was more effective coordination of these bureaus under an officer who would be a single point of contact on logistic matters for the Chief of Naval Operations and the Commandant of the Marine Corps.

3. Assignment to the Chief of Yards and Docks of responsibility for maintenance of buildings, grounds and structures, a responsibility previously diffused.

A fourth change was approved on paper but never really went into effect: establishment of a Fleet Activities Command to be in charge of a variety of shore activities previously under the various naval districts and river commands. This shift threatened elimination of hundreds of commanding officer billets. The heat generated by this possibility rose until the Secretary of the Navy limited the change to two pilot projects.

AIR FORCE. Although the youngest service was not reorganized as fully as the other two, here too there was a major change in structure of logistic activities. The Air Force Systems Command was created in 1961 to manage "the research, development, production, and procurement actions required to place a complete aerospace system in operation." [28] It took over the work of the old Air Research and Development Command (except basic research,

---

[28] *Air Force Systems Command* (orientation brochure), p. 4.

which went to Air Force Headquarters), plus R & D procurement and contract management functions from the Air Materiel Command. The latter Command then became Air Force Logistics Command.

Personnel Effects of the New Administration

Some close observers of the McNamara administration would dispute the emphasis this chapter has placed on system and organization. They say that the capacities of the people—McNamara, Vance, Morris, Hitch, and many others—"made all the difference." Actually, of course, the change was a function of both people and systems. Executives with the management viewpoints of the new team would naturally feel the need to change the previous systems of organizational relationships, planning, budgeting, and contract administration.

Continuity in the Top Staff

POLITICAL EXECUTIVES. There is no accepted norm for tenure among federal political executives,[29] but it is reasonable to conclude that the McNamara team showed considerable job stability. The top personnel situation in Defense was certainly more stable than that in State. Comparatively few of the DOD changes were attributable to policy differences or to job performance factors.

In addition to the Secretary himself, Hitch and Brown were still on the job in 1965.[30] So was Arthur Sylvester, Assistant Secretary for Public Affairs, a former New Jersey newspaperman. Deputy Secretary Gilpatric returned to his New York law practice after three full years. He was replaced by Cyrus Vance, who had spent a year and a half as General Counsel and a similar period as Secretary of the Army. Vance had been brought into the government at the suggestion of Vice President Lyndon Johnson, who had

---

[29] A study of federal political executives and commissioners is being carried out by David T. Stanley, Dean E. Mann, and Jameson W. Doig at the Brookings Institution.

[30] Hitch resigned in the spring of 1965; Brown was slated to become Secretary of the Air Force in October 1965.

observed his work as counsel to some Senate subcommittees. Morris, Assistant Secretary for Installations and Logistics, worked almost four years, then was succeeded by Paul Ignatius, who had been his "opposite number" in Army and later Under Secretary of the Army.

Another long-termer was Paul Nitze, who spent almost three years as Assistant Secretary for International Security Affairs. Nitze was a former Wall Street investment banker (Dillon, Read) who served in various federal posts concerned with international relations during World War II and the Truman administration. He was Director of the State Department's Policy Planning Staff from 1950 to 1953. Nitze left the ISA job when McNamara picked him for Navy Secretary late in 1963, and was succeeded by William Bundy. After six months Bundy became Assistant Secretary of State for Far Eastern Affairs, and his Defense job went to John T. McNaughton, who had been DOD General Counsel since July 1962. McNaughton, a former Harvard professor, had been working on disarmament matters in the Office of the Secretary of Defense.

There was more of a problem with the key job of Assistant Secretary for Manpower held by Carlisle P. Runge, a Wisconsin law professor. Although Runge was well liked in the Pentagon, he had difficulty adapting to the high-speed, numbers-heavy McNamara approach.[31] He resigned in July 1962 and was replaced by Norman Paul, the Secretary's legislative assistant.

In the military departments there was turnover in the jobs of Army and Navy Secretary, but otherwise a fairly stable situation. Elvis Stahr, who had left the presidency of the University of West Virginia to become Secretary of the Army, resigned in July 1962 to head the University of Indiana. Stahr issued a statement criticizing the centralization of decision-making under McNamara.[32] He insisted that this statement not be construed as a "parting blast," but it could hardly be construed otherwise. Vance was then Secretary until the end of 1963, when Stephen Ailes, a Washington lawyer who had been Under Secretary since 1961, stepped up.

[31]*Sunday Star* (Washington), July 29, 1962.
[32] *New York Times,* July 8, 1962.

At Navy John Connally, a Texan closely associated with Lyndon Johnson, served as Secretary only a year before resigning to run successfully for Governor of Texas. His successor was a Fort Worth lawyer and banker named Fred Korth, who had been Assistant Secretary of the Army under Truman. Korth now served two years before he resigned "to attend to personal and family affairs." He had been criticized in the press for writing letters about the business of a Fort Worth bank on Navy stationery. As noted earlier, he was succeeded by Paul Nitze, who enjoyed the confidence of McNamara and of the White House staff.

Air Force Secretary Eugene Zuckert remained on the job until the fall of 1965. The under secretaries and assistant secretaries of the military departments served on the average at least two years.

CAREER STAFF. The attitudes of top military career officers toward the new Pentagon management can be characterized as a mixture of disciplined obedience, cautious cooperation, appreciation of the executive capacities and analytical skills of the civilian leaders, and apprehension about the changes in the power structure. For the most part any resistance to the new way of doing business was covert, although it was apparent that some officers' views were being expressed by sympathetic Congressmen, as in the row over the B-70 bomber. The attitude of the administration toward overt recalcitrance was reflected in two top-level cases. Admiral George Anderson, selected as Chief of Naval Operations early in the Kennedy administration, was not reappointed at the end of his two-year term but was made Ambassador to Portugal. This was generally interpreted as reprisal for the Admiral's resistant attitude toward the Secretary of Defense. (He had testified in opposition to McNamara's position on the TFX airplane controversy.) The Air Force Chief of Staff, General Curtis LeMay, another officer who had disagreed with McNamara's policies, was given a one-year extension of his term to 1964.

The key military figure of the Kennedy administration was General Maxwell Taylor. After retiring as Army Chief of Staff in 1959, Taylor had published a book, *The Uncertain Trumpet*, in which he urged improvement of conventional warfare capabilities and advocated a single Defense chief of staff. He was appointed military adviser to President Kennedy after the Cuba fiasco in

1961 and then Chairman of the Joint Chiefs of Staff a year later. President Johnson made him Ambassador to Vietnam in 1964, after sending McNamara himself on a series of missions to investigate the very difficult military and diplomatic situation in that country. Taylor's successor as Chairman of the Joint Chiefs was General Earle Wheeler, former Army Chief of Staff.

In general the top military officers and career civilian officials supplied the expert continuity expected of them. Most turnover was attributable to normal retirement or career movement, and those who left were succeeded by qualified officers or civilians from the bureaucracies. There was one notable exception among the civilians. John Dillon, Administrative Assistant to the Secretary of the Navy, retired after Secretary Nitze had reduced the scope of his job by giving important organization responsibilities to a new man from industry, Howard Merrill, who had been Vice President for Administration of the Martin Marietta Corporation.

Personnel Administration

The work of the Assistant Secretary for Manpower did not have nearly as great an impact upon the military departments as did the work of the Comptroller or the Assistant Secretary for Installations and Logistics. This was to be expected. The Army, Navy, and Air Force kept their separate identities as employers of both military and civilian personnel, although the Office of the Secretary of Defense continued to press for uniform policies. In both categories morale and presumably personnel retention were improved by substantial salary increases enacted for military personnel in 1963 and for civilian employees in 1962 and 1964. Other major personnel concerns included progress in nondiscrimination policies, efforts to improve the retention rates of junior officers, and placement of civilian employees affected by closing of military installations.

Changes in the Reserve

McNamara's willingness to maim sacred political cows in his efforts to increase military readiness at reduced costs was again shown by his reorganization of the Army Reserve and the National

Guard. First revealed in June 1961,[33] his plan was fought over in appropriations hearings in the spring of 1962 and put into effect in December of that year. Four Reserve divisions and four National Guard divisions were eliminated, and there was a net decrease of 800 smaller units as a result of sweeping adjustments. Eight combat-ready Reserve brigades replaced the divisions that were eliminated. Political concessions had been made, however. The Secretary had dropped a plan to cut the Army Reserves from 700,000 to 642,000 and to eliminate sixteen National Guard armories.

Two years later an even more drastic change was announced: a further drastic reduction in Army Reserves and strengthening of high-priority (i.e., more combat-ready) National Guard units. The Secretary's order stopped all Army reservists from receiving pay for their drills. A month later it was announced that merger of the Air Force Reserves into the Air National Guard was being recommended by the Air Staff.

Viewing the McNamara Take-Over

The rapid pace and analytically centralized approach of the McNamara team have already endured more than four years without loss of purpose or momentum. One Brookings interviewee was a poor prophet when he remarked in June 1961, "There is a limit to human endurance, and the amount of work McNamara is demanding of his subordinates is bound to diminish in time." In the military departments there has been increasing acceptance in general of the new way of doing business, despite objections to specific decisions that run counter to the interests or judgment of key officials.

The new team has also enjoyed generally good (though ambivalent) congressional relations. Representative Carl Vinson, who spoke on military matters with more authority and background than any other member of the House, called McNamara the greatest Secretary of Defense.[34] Vinson earlier had fought

[33] *Washington Post,* June 3, 1961.

[34] Rowland Evans, Jr., "The Sixth Sense of Carl Vinson," *The Reporter,* Vol. 26 (April 12, 1962), p. 26.

McNamara to a standstill over the B-70 and yielded only under personal pressure by President Kennedy. Similarly many a member of Congress who applauded the administration of the Department of Defense complained about the TFX decision, or about closing an installation, or about a threatened Army Reserve unit.

The department has also enjoyed generally favorable press relations. There have been some complaints of "managing the news," based on what seemed to the press unduly selective policies in releasing information, and criticisms of "censorship" of speeches or articles by high military officers.[35] Such problems are inevitable, however, in the relationship between a free press and military management, and objections of this type can be expected in any administration. The press resists any restrictions on its access to information, and Defense officials want to restrict release of any information that could conceivably aid an enemy or undermine confidence in the management of American military affairs. Each side's attitude puts a healthy sort of pressure on the other, and the resulting equilibrium is only occasionally broken by controversy.

Criticism of OSD Controls

There has been thoughtful criticism of the size, strength, and appetite for detail of the OSD bureaucracy. Such criticism questions whether the degree of centralized decision-making now in effect is realistic, considering the size and variety of the services' functions. In particular the critics note that the review-and-concurrence procedures diffuse responsibility and delay action.[36] They also say that in an attempt to achieve "perfection on paper," worthwhile developmental work is discouraged and the desirable attributes of interservice rivalry are ignored.[37]

Such criticisms tend to ignore the difficulty of pinpointing responsibility under the previous system. They also underrate two key factors: the need for coordination of national security policy and the total size of the military budget. The close relationship

[35] See, for example, Jack Raymond, "Pentagon Blocks Defense Articles," *New York Times*, Oct. 11, 1961.

[36] See John C. Ries, *The Management of Defense* (The Johns Hopkins Press, 1964); and Hanson W. Baldwin, "Slow-Down in the Pentagon," *Foreign Affairs*, Vol. 43 (January 1965), pp. 262–80.

[37] Baldwin, *op. cit.*, p. 275 ff.

of military force structures and readiness planning to foreign policy objectives requires effective control of programming by the Secretary of Defense. The enormous costs of modern weapons systems also require such control if military expenditures are to be kept within rational limits in an era when development of a single system may cost $20 billion.

Another implied criticism, frequently and casually uttered, states that "only a McNamara" can effectively use the present methods of doing business. Granting that future Secretaries of Defense may not match Mr. McNamara's capacity for handling detail, it still seems both unlikely and undesirable that the department will return to earlier methods of programming, budgeting, and logistical coordination. Nor can it be expected to reduce its emphasis on cost effectiveness studies. Assistant Secretary Hitch summarizes the situation well:

> . . . I cannot imagine a Defense Secretary who would willingly forego the assurance, provided by the new planning-programming-budgeting system, that his military plans are in proper balance and that the budgets he proposes actually provide the capabilities that his military planners are counting on. As President Truman pointed out at the end of World War II in his Message to the Congress proposing a single Department of Defense: ". . . strategy, program and budget are all aspects of the same basic decisions."[38]

Plus Factors in This Transition

The new team in 1961 got off to a fast start with excellent co-operation from its predecessors and from the career staff. Secretary McNamara and his assistants identified clear objectives that were part of President Kennedy's program. They used methods of planning and administration that were in conformity with both common sense and advanced management doctrine, notably the Five Year Force Structure and Financial Program, the cost effectiveness studies, and the Cost Reduction Program. They displayed both high competence and unusual energy. Their success was also aided by the period in which they arrived. There was wide recog-

[38] Remarks of Assistant Secretary Hitch, *op. cit.*, p. 15.

nition, after some fourteen years of looser management of the department, that the time was ripe, perhaps overripe, for a more centralized approach. Future times will test and could conceivably alter or destroy the present system. After four years, however, the organization and management style of the McNamara team is recognized as a success—a success shared by all who supported them, at the White House, in the military and civilian bureaucracies, and in Congress.

4 / DEPARTMENT OF THE INTERIOR
New Advances on Old Frontiers

> Thus it is our task in our time and in our generation to
> hand down undiminished to those who come after us, as
> was handed down to us by those who went before, the
> natural wealth and beauty which is ours . . .
>
> —President Kennedy
> Remarks at Dedication Ceremonies of
> the National Wildlife Federation
> Building, March 3, 1961

IN THE INTERIOR Department—that sector
of the New Frontier most concerned with America's frontiers in
a physical sense—the transition to the Kennedy administration
followed a different pattern from that in State and Defense. The
change was neither a smooth take-over by men who had been
there before nor a jolting start by hard-driving management experts. It was rather a series of new advances on old program
fronts managed with energy and political astuteness. It was not
characterized by large-scale changes in organization or personnel
administration.

The change-over reflected in large measure the personality and
experience of the new Secretary, Stewart L. Udall, an athletic
young lawyer from Tucson, Arizona, who had served three terms
in the House of Representatives and had been on the Interior and
Insular Affairs Committee. He had represented a district whose
principal concerns involved major programs of the Interior De-

partment: Indians, public lands, conservation, water, parks and outdoor recreation. He was well prepared, then, for a diverse and difficult job. As the *Washington Post* commented editorially:

> The Interior assignment will be no pushover. Manifold and mammoth problems of resources development and protection of water sources, pollution abatement and recreational demand, await the new administrator. The outgoing Secretary Seaton has conducted Interior affairs even handedly and fairly, but initiative has been badly handicapped by philosophical and budgetary limitations of the Eisenhower Administration. Mr. Udall will find a more sympathetic philosophy and a more liberal budget, but Federal funds will be by no means inexhaustible.[1]

"Keeping in Touch" Politically

The new Secretary never really broke his ties with Congress but made use of his official and personal connections with Capitol Hill to push his department's programs. During the six weeks between the announcement of his appointment and Inauguration Day he was swamped both with preparations for his new job and with work from his congressional office. One of his early acts as Secretary was to sit down informally with the chairmen of the Senate and House Interior Committees to discuss a variety of policy matters, and he maintained a heavy schedule of congressional contacts, both formal and informal, over the next four years. He maintained another link with his old constituency when his younger brother and law partner, Morris K. Udall, succeeded to his House seat and his place on the Interior Committee.

Key Appointments

President-elect Kennedy gave Udall a fairly free hand on appointments, and the Secretary's choices reflected a strong concern for congressional relations and for contacts with important constituencies. The new Under Secretary was James K. Carr, a pro-

[1] Dec. 8, 1960.

fessional water and power engineer from California who had worked for the Bureau of Reclamation, the House Interior Committee, and the State of California. Carr did not serve as the "general manager" or "alter ego" type of Number Two man, but concerned himself with western power and water problems so faithfully that he was informally referred to by some within the department as the "Secretary from California."

The Assistant Secretary for Public Land Management, John A. Carver, Jr., had been for four years administrative assistant to Senator Frank Church of Idaho. Carver's new responsibilities included the National Park Service, the Bureau of Indian Affairs, the Office of Territories, the Alaska Railroad, and the Bureau of Land Management.[2]

The other assistant secretaries were also close to politicians and clienteles. Former Senator Frank Briggs of Missouri, the Assistant Secretary for Fish and Wildlife, was suggested by the National Wildlife Federation and endorsed by former President Truman. The Assistant Secretary for Water and Power, Kenneth Holum, had been active in the field of public power as well as a state legislator in South Dakota. The job of Assistant Secretary for Mineral Resources went to John M. Kelly, a New Mexico oil producer who had served as state geologist. D. Otis Beasley, a longtime career man serving as Administrative Assistant Secretary, had close official and personal ties with Representative Michael Kirwan, chairman of the appropriations subcommittee handling Interior's funds.

Bureau Chiefs and Others

Similar sensitivity was shown in some bureau chief appointments. Named chief of the Bureau of Land Management was Karl Landstrom of the staff of the House Interior Committee. Landstrom had been for many years in career jobs in the field of

---

[2] At Interior, as at State and Agriculture, each assistant secretary (except for the administrative assistant secretary) is a line official in charge of several bureaus. At Defense and at Health, Education, and Welfare, assistant secretaries serve in a staff capacity.

resource management in the Interior and Agriculture Departments. For Director of the Office of Territories, a native of Guam, Richard F. Taitano, was selected. Udall retained Floyd Dominy, who had been Commissioner of Reclamation at the end of the Eisenhower administration. Dominy had built effective congressional relationships, particularly with Senator Carl Hayden of Arizona, President Pro Tem of the Senate. Other bureau chiefs held over included the Director of the Bureau of Mines, M. J. Ankeny, who enjoyed the confidence of the United Mine Workers; Conrad Wirth, Director of the National Park Service; and Thomas Nolan, Director of the Geological Survey. The new Fish and Wildlife Commissioner, Clarence Pautzke, was a professional game and fish specialist from Washington State and Alaska.

In the Bureau of Indian Affairs, which has always posed difficult problems of politics and policy, the new administration moved slowly. John O. Crow, a Chippewa Indian and veteran official of the bureau, was appointed Acting Commissioner. Meanwhile Udall named an expert four-man Task Force on Indian Affairs (whose findings are outlined later in the chapter). After the Task Force had filed its report in July 1961 one of its members, Philleo Nash, was made Commissioner. Nash, a professional anthropologist, was a long-time student of Indian matters. He had been an assistant to President Truman, Lieutenant Governor of Wisconsin, and was an active political supporter of Senator Hubert Humphrey of Minnesota.

The Southwest was represented in two key legal appointments: Max N. Edwards of New Mexico, recommended by Senator Clinton Anderson, was made Legislative Counsel, and Frank J. Barry, Jr., of Tucson, a friend and law partner of Udall, was appointed Solicitor.

For the important post of Director of the Technical Review Staff Udall selected Charles H. Stoddard, a professional forester, resources economist, and conservationist.

Other 1961 appointments could be enumerated, but they would only confirm the general pattern: men both professionally qualified and acceptable to the department's political supporters and constituencies.

The Udall Approach at the Start

The new leadership at Interior was not only politically realistic and responsive, but showed brisk leadership in efforts to improve conservation and resource programs. The Secretary in particular showed that he felt personally involved in such causes as wilderness preservation and outdoor recreation improvement. He also worked hard for water pollution abatement—a function primarily of the Department of Health, Education, and Welfare, but involving many of Interior's activities.

Politics on the Side

Udall also felt personally involved in partisan political matters outside the department's programs, especially during his first months in office. His political interest was manifested by phone calls to congressmen to build support for the Kennedy-Rayburn plan to expand the House Rules Committee and by a public statement interpreted as blaming Republicans for the "Bay of Pigs" blunder.

His reputation as an energetic Democratic partisan was untidily strengthened when an oil lobbyist, J. K. Evans, used Udall's name to urge Washington oil and gas men to buy tickets to a Jefferson-Jackson Day dinner. Udall seemed tardy in disavowing this pressure, and he was in trouble with the Republicans, the President, and the press for a few days in May 1961.[3]

After that his political energy was channeled into support of his department's programs, and he enjoyed generally favorable public relations. He accepted speaking engagements throughout the country and held frequent and very frank conferences with reporters.

Taking Over From the Outgoing Administration

In getting started on their job of program leadership the Udall team, like most new political executives in 1961, were helped by their predecessors. Books of information were prepared and

[3] New York Times, May 3, 4, 1961; Washington Post, May 3, 4, 6, 1961.

handed over, and briefing sessions were held on pending problems. This Republican-Democratic duet, however, seems to have featured correct words but dubious harmonies. There was an undercurrent of reluctance and resistance on both sides, attributed by some officials to outgoing Secretary Fred Seaton's severe disappointment with the 1960 election results and to the wish of the Udall group to avoid premature policy commitments. Until Inauguration Day the career staff naturally took their cues from the outgoing political executives and refrained from giving the new group as much help as they could have given, and wanted to give. The careerists were permitted to discuss organizational and procedural subjects but were required to clear any discussions of substantive program topics with the designated liaison man in the Secretary's office, who in turn reported them to the White House.

Seaton met for lunch with Udall the day after the latter's selection was announced and gave him a book containing summaries of department policies and problems. He did *not* show him the department's budget submission for fiscal year 1962. Udall was given office space and worked at Interior from early January on. He concentrated less on policy problems, however, than he did on interviewing candidates for top jobs and on leftover business from his congressional office. Meanwhile, the incoming assistant secretaries were briefed by the career people and given appropriate material. A summary of current problems in the department, prepared by the Bureau of the Budget, was also available.

In general, as one of Udall's assistants told the author, the new team "had no complaint" about help from their predecessors. Nevertheless, the process of handing over useful information was deficient both in energy and in goodwill, compared with what was happening at the Departments of State and Defense.

Policy Signposts

The directions of the policy advances that Udall and his staff wished to make were in many respects well-marked. Two principal guides were the Democratic platform and the report of one of the pre-inaugural task forces, the Kennedy-Johnson Natural Resources Advisory Committee, a group of 450 chaired by Congressman Frank E. Smith of Mississippi. These guides were followed by President Kennedy's message to Congress of February 23, 1961, on natural resources, an explicit and comprehensive list of objectives. Goals of primary interest to the Department of the Interior included:

Better coordination of resource planning by the Executive Office of the President

Ending the Eisenhower "no new starts" policy, which had blocked new reclamation projects

Development of major river basin plans

Strengthened and accelerated flood control measures

Extension of research in saline water conversion

Continued development of public electric power projects and of cooperative marketing arrangements with private power companies

Better balanced usage of public lands heretofore used mainly for grazing

More aggressive programs to develop and market timber from public lands

Protection of wilderness areas

Formulation of a comprehensive outdoor recreation program

Development of seashore park areas [4]

Meanwhile the Task Force on Indian Affairs was making its studies. This group was headed by W. W. Keeler, head of the Oklahoma Cherokee tribe and an oil company executive. Other members were Philleo Nash, soon to be named Commissioner of Indian Affairs; James Officer, an anthropologist and official of the Bureau of Indian Affairs; and William Zimmerman, a former BIA Assistant Commissioner. The Task Force Report, released in the summer of 1961, urged a shift of emphasis away from the Eisenhower administration's policy of terminating trust relationships to Indians. The Task Force recommended instead greater development of human and natural resources on Indian reservations, including better education and credit facilities. There were other recommendations to better the legal, economic, and social

[4] *New York Times*, Feb. 24, 1961.

standing of Indians. The report found, however, that eligibility for special federal services should be withdrawn from Indians whose education and incomes enable them to look after their own affairs.[5]

Commenting in oversimplified terms on policy changes in 1961, one official interviewed (a career man) said that the main effort of the previous administration was "to keep the Government out of things," and of the new group, to get into them: in short, a more active federal role in resource planning and management.

This theme ran through another major policy pronouncement, President Kennedy's message to Congress on conservation, March 1, 1962. The President stressed the need for expansion of outdoor recreation areas, reiterated earlier policy statements on water, power, and public land management, and urged increased research and development work on minerals, water, and fish and wildlife projects. Most of these themes were reemphasized in a White House Conference on Conservation in May 1962.

Program Developments

Some of the program developments of Udall's administration represented further progress toward long-held policy objectives. Some were considerable modifications of the previous administration's policies. Some were brand-new. Space permits mention of only a few examples.

Water and Power

The new administration recommended and Congress approved expansions of the reclamation program, notably large-scale irrigation projects in Colorado and New Mexico. One, the "Fryingpan-Arkansas" project, was to divert water from the west slope of the Rockies to the east slope for irrigation, flood control, and power generation purposes. Farther east, the federal government entered into an agreement with the states of Delaware, New Jersey,

[5] *1961 Annual Report of the Secretary of the Interior*, pp. 277–78.

New York, and Pennsylvania for comprehensive development of the water resources of the Delaware River Basin. (Udall was concerned with Interior's "image" as a "western" department and was eager to develop conservation and recreation projects in the East.)

Meanwhile federal research and demonstration work in desalting water was expanded both by construction of new demonstration plants and by increased "R&D" contract awards, and the costs of producing fresh water under this program went steadily downward. In 1964 a new Water Resources Research Act authorized federal grants to state universities for research on critical problems of water supply.

In the electric power field the department continued to increase generating capacity, but the principal policy emphasis was on transmission and marketing arrangements to help assure the best utilization of power from all sources. Secretary Udall, somewhat to the dismay of public power advocates who had supported the Kennedy cause, entered into a variety of arrangements with privately owned electric utilities. One provided for coordination of generation and storage facilities in the Pacific Northwest. Another was an agreement with private utilities to build some of the transmission lines for power generated on the Colorado River. Still another, "the Pacific Coast intertie," was a proposal to link the Northwest and the Southwest so that surplus power from the Bonneville Power Administration could be used in Southern California. Congress voted the necessary funds in 1964.

Recreation and Parks

Efforts in the department to increase recreation facilities were strengthened by the report of the Outdoor Recreation Resources Review Commission, appointed near the end of the Eisenhower administration. One of its recommendations, creation of a Bureau of Outdoor Recreation to coordinate federal programs affecting outdoor recreation and to help state and local governments and private industries working in this field, was put into effect by Secretary Udall. Congress later passed legislation to define the federal government's responsibilities in outdoor recreation. New legislation in 1964 also authorized a new Land and Water Conservation Fund, a revolving fund that receives fees paid by the public using recreational facilities and spends the money for purchase and development of new recreational areas. Meanwhile the National Park Service pressed ahead with its "Mission 66" program for improvement of facilities, and several new parks and monuments were authorized by Congress each year.

Land Management

During his first month in office the new Secretary ordered an eighteen-month moratorium on public land entry applications. During this period the staff of the Bureau of Land Management reduced a large backlog of applications and began a comprehensive inventory, evaluation, and classification of lands so that each type of land could be planned for best use. These studies led to submission of legislation to modernize the public land laws, disposing of lands not needed for public purposes.[6] The general policy was to encourage well-planned multiple use of lands for recreation, mineral resources, and forestry. This contrasted with what the new administration thought was a previous overemphasis on use of the lands for grazing.

Minerals

There was prompt action also in the department's work concerned with mineral resources. The program to buy and store helium gas was expanded. The new Office of Coal Research, created near the end of the Eisenhower administration, began contracting out research and development work on new ways to transport and use coal. The Office of Minerals Mobilization, an emergency stockpile planning organization, was expanded and renamed the Office of Minerals and Solid Fuels. In all offices and bureaus concerned with minerals, exploration and research activities were increased.

[6] Bills providing for multiple use management and for public sale.

Fish and Wildlife

There was a similar trend in the fish and wildlife area. There was research, for example, on manufacture and use of fish protein concentrates, on effects of industrial pollution and of pesticides on wildlife, and on propagation and migration of fish and birds. New wildlife refuges were opened and fish hatcheries expanded.

Indian Affairs; Territories

The same developmental vigor prevailed in the Bureau of Indian Affairs, which had an additional stimulus, the 1961 Task Force report. A new Division of Economic Development was created to bring together the bureau's resource functions (agricultural assistance, forestry, real estate appraisals, real property management, road construction and maintenance) with industrial development and the revolving credit program. Work began on area redevelopment studies and on a large Navajo irrigation project. Tribal industrial ventures of many kinds increased. Educational development was highlighted by the publicity given ten young Indians and Eskimos from Alaska who were going home to good jobs after completing training in electronics in New York City. Meanwhile school construction was accelerated, and enrollment increased. Technical and vocational training was greatly expanded. Finally, federal housing programs were started on Indian reservations for the first time.

At the same time educational and economic development and political improvements went ahead in the American territories. The Territory of Guam needed extra help to recover from the effects of two devastating typhoons in 1962 and 1963, but these disasters stimulated more realistic and modern planning of community facilities than would otherwise have occurred.

Legislative Plus Executive Progress

The department's programs generally were invigorated by the new leadership. Congress responded well on the whole with both appropriations and with program legislation to meet the needs which the Secretary kept emphasizing to the public and to appropriate interest groups, as well as to the congressional committees. His efforts reached a real payoff point near the end of the 88th Congress when a group of important Interior bills were enacted: the "wilderness bill," the Pacific Coast power intertie, the act establishing the Land and Water Conservation Fund, the Commercial Fisheries Research and Development Act, and many others. The Secretary, according to his assistants, cheerfully accepted the extra burden of frequent visits to the White House to attend signing ceremonies.

Administering the Department

Despite the fact that these program developments were carried on by an organization of some 69,000 employees with a budget of $1.2 billion (fiscal year 1965), the Secretary showed little overt concern with matters of organization, personnel administration, and finance.[7] There were in fact relatively few changes and problems in these respects—considering the size of the department and the dynamic nature of its programs.

Organization

The Secretary of the Interior, unlike the Secretaries of State and Defense, did not commission a "fresh look" study of the department's organization. As the Kennedy administration came to power, a few rumors buzzed around Washington that the idea of a new, broader "Department of Resources" was being considered. This notion raised the possibility of a struggle with such politically powerful and bureaucratically able groups as the Corps of Engineers and the Forest Service. If Kennedy and Udall considered this (and reliable sources say they did), the idea never saw the

[7] Yet the comment of a well-informed and otherwise sympathetic observer that "Udall's major liability is that he is no administrator and never will be" seems over-severe. Helene C. Monberg, "Stewart Udall Enhances Interior's Mission," *Gallup, N.M., Daily Independent*, Dec. 21, 1964—a well-researched, comprehensive review of Udall's work 1961-1964.

light of day. The new team carried on with the same simple functional organization that they had inherited.

The department had been for many years a loose confederation of strong bureaus, each with a strong constituency and a stable career staff—notably the Park Service, Indian Affairs, Geological Survey, Reclamation, and the Bureau of Mines. Under the Udall administration this situation changed, yet it remained the same. It remained the same in the sense that the bureaus maintained all their old ties and continued and expanded their programs. The situation changed primarily in these respects: (1) The bureaus were now represented to the Congress and to the public by an unusually aggressive, knowledgeable Secretary. (2) Two of the four "program" assistant secretaries, Carver (Public Land Management) and Kelly (Mineral Resources), exerted real supervisory power over their bureaus. They played a stronger part in planning the budget and in coordinating program activities than was customary for Interior's assistant secretaries. (3) More than ever before, the bureaus shared in larger program developments that cut across bureau and even department lines, such as river basin studies, water pollution control, the broad outdoor recreation program, comprehensive land use planning studies, and a broad approach to minerals utilization. Inevitably this change produced some organizational strain, as for example the reluctance of the Director of the National Park Service to be coordinated by a sister group, the new Bureau of Outdoor Recreation. The increased emphasis on broad research and planning for minerals also could be said to have caused underground rumblings in the Bureau of Mines.

RESEARCH AND PLANNING. Although Udall never made a broad organization study, he did commission Resources for the Future [8] to make ". . . a thoroughgoing analysis of the planning, policy making and research functions of this Department." [9] The RFF staff were already generally familiar with department functions, because of their many common interests, and the study was fin-

[8] An independent organization for research and education in the development, conservation, and use of natural resources.

[9] *A Report on Planning, Policy Making, and Research Activities—U. S. Department of the Interior* (Resources for the Future, Inc., 1961), p. v.

ished within a few months. The recommendations of the brief (thirty-eight-page) report fell into three categories:

Scientific research and planning: Appointment of a Science Adviser to the Secretary and strengthening of coordinated scientific research programs.

Economic research: Expanded studies of the economics of natural resources—supply and demand, investments, regional aspects. Such studies were to be led and coordinated by an Economics Adviser to the Secretary.

General improvement of planning and decision-making processes: Effective definition of responsibilities, planning, goal-setting, staffing, and communication in the Office of the Secretary; also re-examination of the bureaus' program-planning functions.[10]

The report was helpful but did not have a strong impact. The position of Science Adviser was established. The first two incumbents, Roger Revelle and John C. Calhoun, were originally more concerned about relationships with the White House and with other departments than about internal programs, but Calhoun did become deeply involved in planning water research. There was little progress toward the broad economic studies which the RFF report suggested be made in the Office of the Secretary.

There was more activity, however, in program planning, more or less in line with the RFF recommendations. The Secretary's Technical Review Staff, which had been reduced in size and given relatively little to do by Secretary Seaton, was renamed the Resources Program Staff, given additional personnel, and encouraged to play a heavier role in program matters affecting various assistant secretaries and bureaus. This group, for example, represented the Secretary in dealing with the Outdoor Recreation Resources Review Commission and did the staff work in planning the functions of the new Bureau of Outdoor Recreation. They were also responsible for work on the Land and Water Conservation Fund Act and on the Job Corps under President Johnson's "poverty program." This staff is used by the Secretary as his personal staff on various problems that cannot readily be assigned to other or-

[10] *Ibid.*, esp. pp. 16–17, 20–23, 28–30, and 35–36.

ganizations, e.g., work with the Area Redevelopment Administration, preparation of material for the President's State of the Union Message, and some speechwriting. Eight of its professional staff are stationed in the field to handle interbureau coordination.

NEW ORGANIZATIONS. Although the department's basic organization structure did not change from 1961 to 1965, there were a few additions. The Bureau of Outdoor Recreation, as noted earlier, was created in 1962 and placed under the Assistant Secretary for Public Land Management. There were two changes in the domain of the Assistant Secretary for Mineral Resources. The Office of Coal Research, authorized by Congress in July 1960, began its work of finding new ways to dig, carry, and use coal. The Office of Minerals and Solid Fuels was set up as a renamed and strengthened successor to the Office of Minerals Mobilization in the field of mobilization stockpile planning. Another mobilization planning body, the Defense Electric Power Administration, was literally reincarnated. First set up in 1950, it was abolished in 1953 and reestablished in 1962 to do emergency planning for electric power resources.

Personnel

Secretary Udall made a good impression on the career staff of the department at the beginning. In a brief speech a few days after the 1961 inauguration he commended their spirit and dedication, stressed the importance of their responsibilities, and said that their ideas would be welcomed. This impression was strengthened by Udall's evident belief in the department's goals and his efforts to expand its programs. He and his assistant secretaries also consulted bureau officials on important decisions more than Seaton and his staff had.

Some of this good feeling was spoiled temporarily when the Secretary issued an order that appointments and promotions above routine levels be approved in advance by his office. Another order put some brakes on official travel. The prior approval requirement was understandably interpreted by employees as a possible way to introduce political considerations into career personnel processes. There was adverse publicity,[11] and the order was rescinded after it had been in effect only two months.

Stability in the Top Staff Again

The political executives at Interior, as at Defense, "stayed put" for the most part. The assistant secretaries all served into 1965. John Carver, the assistant secretary with the largest domain—and generally regarded as the strongest—was made Under Secretary early in 1965. Carr, his predecessor, had resigned in July 1964. Administrative Assistant Secretary D. Otis Beasley, a career man, stayed on. There was also relatively little turnover among the bureau chiefs, all of whom were professionally well qualified for their jobs. One notable departure was that of Conrad Wirth, long-time Director of the National Park Service, who retired in January 1964, having evinced resistance to Carver's supervision and to the effect on his bureau of the broadened outdoor recreation policies. Also replaced was the Director of the Bureau of Land Management, Karl Landstrom, who was made an assistant to Udall. He was succeeded by Charles Stoddard, Chief of the Resources Program Staff. The Director of the Office of Territories, Richard Taitano, was replaced by Mrs. Ruth Van Cleve, a career attorney in the department who had long dealt with territorial matters.

Staff members below the level of bureau chief were experienced holdovers. Even in the Solicitor's office, where political turnover might have been expected, two veteran attorneys were kept on in top positions.

Budget

Secretary Udall was no McNamara in terms of a deep interest in financial management, but he was inevitably involved in the major aspects of the budget process, and he did his homework well.

Two months after the 1961 inauguration he requested a budget increase of about $41 million (an increase of about 5 percent) to support some of his program objectives. The largest items in the

[11] *Evening Star* (Washington), Feb. 6 and 9, 1961.

increase were $20 million for Indian school construction; $4 million for land acquisition and $6 million for construction for the Park Service; $3 million for conservation on public lands; $2.5 million for research in the Fish and Wildlife Service; $2.3 million for Bonneville Power Administration transmission facilities.[12] Most of these items were approved.

In succeeding years the department's budgets rose about $100 million each year, and employment rose about 5,000 a year before leveling off in fiscal year 1964:[13]

Fiscal Year	Actual Expenditures (in millions)	Actual Employment
1961	$ 801	59,458
1962	908	64,078
1963	1,029	69,558
1964	1,124	69,867
1965	1,198 (enacted)	68,700 (est.)
1966	1,174 (est.)	70,040 (est.)

The main factors in the rising budget were those mentioned in the discussion of program developments, such as construction of reclamation projects, power lines, and Indian schools; purchase of park lands; conservation work on public lands; and research on water and minerals. The greatly reduced rate of growth in employment resulted in large part from President Johnson's emphasis upon economy.

Relationships and Progress in General

Secretary Udall took over briskly in the beginning. Through the four years that followed he moved ahead with a combination of vigor, goodwill, and belief in the department's purposes that won support from employees, the Congress, the special interest groups, the press, and the public. Both Presidents Kennedy and Johnson were firm supporters of Udall's objectives, although both were too preoccupied with other matters to give close attention to

[12] Interior Department Press Release, March 20, 1961.

[13] Source: *The Budget of the United States Government* for the fiscal years concerned.

Interior programs. Udall felt, however, that he could get support from the White House when he really needed it. Early in 1965, for example, President Johnson sent a strong conservation message to Congress, emphasizing the need to preserve and reclaim natural outdoor beauty spots.

Secretary Udall was able to make these program advances without large organizational changes or wholesale personnel turnover. Thus he found that his department was well adapted to change and progress. His task was made easier by the fact that his policies favored development, reinforcement, expansion of existing programs. He was, in short, driving the department where it wanted to go, and where the Congress was willing for it to go. He and his staff nevertheless exerted vigorous effort, and they deserve credit for significant progress. They took effective command of a going concern and moved it ahead.

THE DEPARTMENT OF AGRICULTURE

New Alphabets, New Policies

American agricultural abundance can be forged into both a significant instrument of foreign policy and a weapon against domestic hardship and hunger. It is no less our purpose to insure that the farm family that produced this wealth will have a parity in income and equality in opportunity with urban families.

—President Kennedy
Message to the Congress on Agriculture,
March 16, 1961

THE 1961 CHANGEOVER at Agriculture had much in common with that at Interior. In each case a large "old-line" department, a loose confederation of strong agencies, with difficult and politically sensitive problems, was taken over by a vigorous young politician with a flair for leadership and public relations. Like Secretary Udall, Secretary Orville L. Freeman was able to make substantial program changes, but in doing so he did more to alter the organization and personnel of his department.

On Inauguration Day 1961 Freeman was not yet forty-three, but he had served three two-year terms as Governor of Minnesota and had been narrowly defeated for a fourth. He was a Minneapolis attorney who had been active in the Democratic-Farmer-Labor Party. In the late forties he had been assistant to Hubert Humphrey when the latter was mayor of Minneapolis.

Freeman's inclination, according to one of his closest associates, was "to sneak in, to move in on his job a little at a time," but he soon found himself moving fast on the whole broad front of farm problems. One reason for this was the attitude of President Kennedy, who said in effect, "Give me the best program you can as soon as you can"—an attitude also reflected in demands by the White House staff for statistics, recommendations, messages. Other reasons were the urgent agricultural problems themselves, such as the piling up of grain surpluses and the decline in farm income.

The hurry-up attitude of the White House was effectively shown on Kennedy's first day in office by his announcement that he had signed an order increasing the quantity and variety of surplus foods for distribution to the needy. Another example came within a month in the form of a proposal for legislation to control the growing surplus of corn and feed grains.[1]

There seemed to have been much less hurry about assembling the new Secretary's top staff, whose members were not announced until the day after inauguration. They included:

Under Secretary Charles S. Murphy, a North Carolinian who had been special counsel to President Truman

Assistant Secretary for Federal-State Relations, Frank J. Welch, Dean of Agriculture at the University of Kentucky, a native Texan

Assistant Secretary for Marketing and Foreign Agriculture, John P. Duncan, Jr., President of the Georgia Farm Bureau Federation

Assistant Secretary for Agricultural Stabilization, James T. Ralph, Director of the California State Department of Agriculture

Director of Agricultural Credit Services (a job equivalent to assistant secretary), John A. Baker, Director of Legislative Services for the National Farmers Union[2]

It was a balanced team. The South was represented, and the Far West, the farm organizations, and agricultural academia, and the

---

[1] *New York Times*, Feb. 16, 1961.
[2] *Washington Post*, Jan. 22, 1961.

President had carried out a campaign commitment to appoint a Midwesterner as Secretary of Agriculture.

The Setting of the Task

Like past political executives in the department, they were moving into a difficult situation with little prospect of pleasing the groups most concerned with it. There was little exaggeration in the comment of one critic:

> Our federally mismanaged agriculture was in its chronic state of growing surpluses, growing reliance on Treasury subsidies, growing dissatisfaction with its results on the part of the farmers themselves, growing resentment by agricultural-exporting countries against our massive export-dumping in the world market; only the patient consumers and taxpayers remained silent and without benefit of effective and dedicated spokesmen.[3]

The problems faced by Freeman's team were of three main types:

1. Vastly increased agricultural productivity—a rise during the 1950's of 80 percent per person engaged in farming. Thus,

2. A heavy and mounting burden of surpluses—the government inventory of wheat grew from 132 million bushels in 1952 to over 1,100 million in 1960; of corn, from 280 million to almost 1,500 million.[4]

3. A sharp drop in farm income—net return to farm operators in 1960 was 26 percent lower than the 1947-49 average.

Policy Commitments and Guidance

The Democratic platform and Kennedy's campaign had urged action along several lines:

Increased use of farm products through greater distribution both in the United States and abroad.

---

[3] Jacob Viner, "Economic Foreign Policy on the New Frontier," *Foreign Affairs*, Vol. 39 (July 1961), p. 560.

[4] *Report of the Secretary of Agriculture 1961*, pp. 1–4.

Stricter controls on production and marketing.

Programs to develop community resources.

More detailed guidance on production and marketing matters appeared in four agricultural task force reports made public by the White House on January 31, 1961. The overall report, "Key Elements of the Agricultural Situation," [5] predicted that farm output would continue to rise more rapidly than consumption and that surpluses would accumulate. The task force noted that "long term agricultural adjustment depends largely on the achievement of a vigorous rate of growth for the rest of the economy and the availability of non-farm jobs." [6] Short-run recommendations emphasized retiring land from production and making participation in land-retirement programs a condition of receiving soil conservation payments. [7]

There were three other task force reports. One on feed grains recommended higher price supports and incentive payments for reducing production. A second, on wheat, proposed a national marketing quota system. The third report dealt with cotton and recommended continuation of the existing export subsidy and price support programs.[8]

Neither the Secretary nor the President committed himself on any of these recommendations, but they were high on the list of matters being studied by the new executives at Agriculture as they began work.

Breaking In

They had many other things to study, too, for they had before them the problem of learning about the structure, program details, finances, personnel, and internal procedures of the department. Freeman's own appointment had been announced December 8,

[5] Prepared by J. N. Efferson, Dean of the Agricultural College, Louisiana State University; Lauren Soth, editorial page editor of the *Des Moines Register and Tribune;* and Jesse W. Tapp, board chairman of the Bank of America.

[6] *New York Times*, Feb. 1, 1961.

[7] *Ibid.* See also "Task Forces Make Recommendations on Farm Problems," *Congressional Quarterly Weekly Report*, Vol. 19 (Feb. 3, 1961), pp. 176–77.

[8] *Ibid.*, p. 177.

and he first conferred with his predecessor, Ezra Taft Benson, on December 20. Benson made a suite of offices available for Freeman's use. Only Freeman and his executive assistant, Thomas R. Hughes, used them before January 1, but some six rooms were in use by staff assistants and advisors by January 20. Nevertheless the Under Secretary and assistant secretaries were not named until the following day, and they had to get acquainted with one another and with the work of the department after they were on the job. The fact that they all had had some experience with the department's programs compensated somewhat for their late start.

Three months before inauguration the career staff had begun work on briefing materials for the new political executives. The staff knew such materials would be needed even if the Republicans won the 1960 election, for Secretary Benson had announced his intention of stepping out. Benson's Administrative Assistant Secretary, Ralph S. Roberts, a career official who had been through the 1953 transition, was the moving spirit behind these preparations. Roberts and his staff worked with representatives of the Bureau of the Budget and the White House to assure that this work was in line with President Eisenhower's policies on transition.

The end products of their efforts were two thick volumes containing about as complete a survival kit for an explorer on the New Frontier as one can imagine. Volume One contained information on:

> The Secretary's authority to determine organization
> Functions, organization, financing, and staffing of all parts of the department
> Internal budget processes and budget items needing attention
> Current legislative matters and congressional liaison information
> Advisory boards and committees
> The security program
> Conflict of interest
> The Rural Development Program
> Defense mobilization planning
> Plans for the department's centennial in 1962

The department's Graduate School

The Farm Credit Administration (an independent agency closely associated with the work of the department)

Volume Two presented biographical information on all officials in the department at or above the level of division chief.

Secretary Benson was well impressed with this material and gave a copy to Freeman. Some twelve to fifteen others went to other new officials. Despite the obvious value of these books they were not used to full advantage. Their sheer bulk deterred their use by busy people who felt that they were running behind as soon as they arrived. Another deterrent was the normal skepticism on the part of new political executives toward advice from the career staff. Thus the latter found themselves answering questions for which they had provided clear answers in the books. There were, however, a few expressions of appreciation for the material, including one from Freeman himself.

Looking back at the take-over nearly four years later, one of Freeman's close associates was asked what had been the most helpful factor in taking control of the department. The answer was interesting: the experience gained in taking over the governorship of Minnesota in 1954—experience in establishing relationships with legislators and with career staff and in planning the main elements of a program.

In timing, the 1961 start compared unfavorably with the 1953 experience. Secretary-designate Benson had toured the country, then met with his National Policy Committee, which included his principal assistants, in December 1952. Soon after, he met with his top team to prepare policy statements which were issued as soon as he took office. It was not possible for Freeman to do this sort of thing because of the late appointment of his Under Secretary and assistant secretaries.

The Personnel To Do the Task

If they were off to a late start, it seemed to be a strong start. As noted earlier, the top political executives were a well-qualified team.

Assistant Secretaries

Under Secretary Murphy was an old Washington hand, and Assistant Secretaries Welch, Duncan, and Ralph were seasoned leaders in the field of agricultural policy. Matters requiring Freeman's attention were organized by two experienced assistants from his Minnesota office, Thomas R. Hughes, his executive assistant, and Mrs. Dorothy H. Jacobson, who worked on legislation and presidential messages. Others in the top group were John A. Baker (already mentioned) as Director of Agricultural Credit Services; Willard W. Cochrane, a Minnesota professor of agricultural economics, whom Freeman brought in to be his chief economic adviser and to head a central economics research organization; and General Counsel John C. Bagwell, a career employee of the Farm Credit Administration.

At the assistant secretary level there was less stability of tenure in Agriculture than at Interior and Defense, but more than at State. The median tenure for the Under Secretary, assistant secretaries, and General Counsel was two and a half years. The Under Secretary and the General Counsel were still on the job after four years. So was Baker, who had been made Assistant Secretary for Rural Development and Conservation in 1962. The other assistant secretaries showed considerable change, partly because of reorganizations (see the next section of this chapter) and partly because of personal career factors. Welch resigned in mid-1962 to become vice president of the Tobacco Institute, and his assistant secretary position was used for Baker's promotion. Duncan resigned in 1963 to become an executive of the Southern Railway at a much higher salary, and his place was taken by George L. Mehren, a University of California professor of agricultural economics.

Assistant Secretary Ralph never got on top of his job in a way that was satisfactory to the Secretary. He was let out in February 1962, amid newspaper stories that he had been on the losing side of a policy dispute in which he favored low subsidies and "self-help" marketing controls, as opposed to high subsidies and mandatory controls.[9] Ralph's stabilization functions were then added to Duncan's duties. Ralph himself was slated to become agricultural

9 *Washington Post,* Feb. 21, 1962; *Evening Star* (Washington), Feb. 24, 1962.

attaché in the Philippines but had not left for that post before he was fired again—this time for having accepted favors from Billie Sol Estes, a Texas speculator who was later convicted of fraud in connection with storage of fertilizer.[10]

The assistant secretary vacancy was used to create a position of Assistant Secretary for International Affairs. This was filled in 1963 by Roland R. Renne, president of Montana State College, who had held several agricultural foreign aid jobs overseas. Renne resigned about a year later and was succeeded by Mrs. Jacobson.

Bureau Chiefs and the "Schedule C's"

In the lower political jobs—agency and bureau heads and "Schedule C" jobs[11]—the Freeman forces made a fairly clean sweep. In the other departments discussed in this book the new secretaries retained a majority of incumbents in such jobs, despite the "political" label on them. Agriculture did not fire them all, but the overturn was greater. The incumbents remained past Inauguration Day but were then asked to leave. A year after inauguration 70 percent of the Schedule C employees in grades GS-13 [12] and above had been replaced.

The Freeman forces kept Richard McArdle as Chief of the Forest Service, Donald Williams as Administrator of the Soil Conservation Service, Byron T. Shaw as Administrator of the Agricultural Research Service, and Alex C. Caldwell as Administrator of the Commodity Exchange Authority.

About a year after the change of administration McArdle retired, following a self-imposed rule of the Forest Service professional corps that its chiefs leave at age 62 to make room for younger men. One factor considered by Secretary Freeman in choosing a successor from among three leading candidates was the quality of a paper prepared by each on a suggested program for the service for the next ten years. His choice was Edward P. Cliff, a thirty-two-year career man in the service.

[10] A conviction reversed on appeal still later because there had been television coverage of the trial.

[11] Positions of a confidential or policy-determining character, whose incumbents may be expected to change in the event of a political transition.

[12] The beginning salary for this grade was $11,150 in 1962, $12,075 in 1964.

Norman M. Clapp, a Wisconsin newspaperman and active Democratic partisan, became head of the Rural Electrification Administration. Howard Bertsch, a former career employee, came back as Administrator of the Farmers Home Administration, after seven years in foreign aid work in Iran. The new Administrator of the Agricultural Stabilization and Conservation Service was Horace D. Godfrey, chief of the North Carolina Agricultural Stabilization and Credit Office. A career employee, S. R. Smith, became Administrator of the Agricultural Marketing Service, and another civil servant, E. T. York, Jr., was made head of the Extension Service. Thus in this transition, as in previous ones, the political chiefs of the department did not hesitate to appoint careerists to political jobs; they just wanted to choose their own careerists.

The Career Staff

This desire led to the immediate replacement of the Administrative Assistant Secretary, Ralph S. Roberts, despite his earnest efforts to smooth the path of the new administration. Roberts had worked for the department more than twenty years and had been in this job for most of the Benson administration. The fact that, like Benson, he was a Mormon from Utah counted heavily against him. Probably a stronger factor was Freeman's belief that the top administrative man is inevitably concerned with policy and that Roberts therefore was identified with Benson's policies.[13] Roberts was "frozen out" from the time Freeman arrived and soon transferred to the Department of State as a Deputy Assistant Secretary for Administration.

In Roberts' place Freeman first designated Claude Baldwin, a career civilian official of the Air Force, but Baldwin's usefulness was impaired by unfavorable publicity about the Roberts move and by allegations that he was in the job because his wife and Mrs. Freeman were friends. He went to a Capitol Hill job, and

[13] This is a defensible view, but one apparently not shared by secretaries of comparable departments covered in this study. Secretary Udall kept Otis Beasley; and Secretary Ribicoff of Health, Education, and Welfare retained Rufus Miles (see Chapter 6). For discussions of careerists' involvement in program policy, see Marver Bernstein, *The Job of the Federal Executive* (Brookings Institution, 1958).

was replaced by Joseph M. Robertson, who had been Freeman's Commissioner of Taxation in Minnesota. All this happened in the first five weeks of the new administration.

Meanwhile the department's Director of Personnel, Ernest C. Betts, another Benson choice, also moved on to the Department of State; he was succeeded by Carl B. Barnes, a career employee.[14] These events contributed to the traditional and inevitable suspicion with which the career staff and new political executives regard one another. (In an inelegant simile suggested by one high Agriculture official, "They go around sniffing each other like dogs.") The civil servants' attitude was aggravated by a temporary order that all promotions to jobs in grades GS-9 and above (then $6,435) be cleared with the Secretary's office. The career staff feared political patronage, and the political executives said they were merely blocking empire-building and top-heavy organization.[15]

Gradually the atmosphere improved. One factor was a series of meetings with employees in which the new Secretary (a former chairman of the Minneapolis Civil Service Commission) emphasized his high regard for the career staff and his dependence upon them.[16] Employees who had been there in 1953 compared this with a wrong start by Benson, who had approved a ham-handed memo implying that employees had better get to work now. Freeman also made a point of introducing himself to employees he met in the corridors. He and Under Secretary Murphy won the confidence of the administrators of services, partly through brief daily staff meetings conducted in a frank and friendly manner. Another healing influence was Robertson himself, a genial executive with impressive experience in public administration. And then there was the sheer passage of time, as men of competence and goodwill learned to work together.

Over the next four years the department's personnel program under Robertson and Barnes continued to stress good relationships with professional staff and improvements in recruitment and training activities.

[14] Benson had also replaced a director of personnel when he took office.
[15] *Evening Star* (Washington), March 21, 1961.
[16] *Washington Post*, Feb. 3, 1961.

By and large the new Secretary of Agriculture chose tested people with experience in the department's programs. The number of changes made in key personnel cannot be considered unreasonable, although the overturn in "Schedule C's" was greater than that in any of the other departments discussed in this book. One of the political executives (an agricultural expert himself), interviewed late in 1964, was asked how the 1961 transition could have been improved. He said that more confidence should have been placed in the career staff from the very start.

New Emphasis in Organization

Political and career staff both were aligned and realigned more than once during the four years to strengthen Secretary Freeman's control of the department and, more importantly, to give more emphasis and visibility to some of his programs. These changes contrasted with the situation at the Interior Department, where Secretary Udall promoted new program activities with substantially the same organization he inherited.

Economics to the Top

Freeman's first change, accomplished only a month after the 1961 inauguration, was to set up an agricultural economics group, headed by an official on the same organizational level as the assistant secretaries. This step was tantamount to reestablishment of the old Bureau of Agricultural Economics. The BAE had been cut and dismembered by Congress in the mid-forties as a result of the unpalatability of its cotton price predictions,[17] attacks by the Farm Bureau Federation (with aid and comfort from "action agencies" in the department), and resentment by southern congressmen of some racial overtones in a community survey in Mississippi.[18] When Secretary Benson took office he abolished the

[17] One is reminded of rulers of ancient primitive societies who beheaded messengers who brought them bad news.

[18] This story is told in some detail in C. M. Hardin, "The BAE Under Fire: A Study in Valuation Conflicts," *Journal of Farm Economics*, Vol. 28 (August 1946), pp. 635–68.

bureau and distributed its reporting functions to the Agricultural Marketing Service and its remaining research functions to the Agricultural Research Service.

Freeman and Willard Cochrane, his Director of Agricultural Economics, who had been his economic adviser in Minnesota, now placed the reporting functions in a new Statistical Reporting Service. A brother service, Economic Research, was set up to include research activities from the Agricultural Marketing Service, the Agricultural Research Service, and other agencies. Both new services reported to Cochrane, as did a small overhead group of staff economists, who were to work on urgent policy questions for the Secretary, like the 1961 feed grain problem. One of these economists, John A. Schnittker, a Kansas State University professor and former staff member of the Council of Economic Advisers, succeeded Cochrane when he resigned in 1964.

In sum, these new organizations put statistical and research tools nearer the Secretary and gave him staff specialists to work on new programs. They also gave the field of agricultural economics more recognition in the department—a matter of concern to members of that profession ever since the Bureau of Agricultural Economics went into its decline.

Another early change was renaming of the Commodity Stabilization Service as the Agricultural Stabilization and Conservation Service in June 1961.

Shifting Services for Program Emphasis

The other principal organization changes in the department consisted of shuffles and reshuffles of the large operating agencies, usually called services or administrations. Although these agencies report to line assistant secretaries who supervise related groups of functions, they operate with considerable independence. Many of them have powerful constituencies in the states (Soil Conservation Service, Extension Service) or in the industrial groups they service (Forest Service, Rural Electrification Administration). Except for the newly centralized and upgraded research and statistical work, Secretary Freeman made no changes in them at the start of his administration.

The departure of Assistant Secretaries Ralph and Welch in 1962 made it easy for Freeman to adjust organization structure to correspond with program emphases. Primarily he wanted to strengthen the rural areas development program and to make sure that forestry and conservation activities were coordinated with it. So Baker, the Director of Agricultural Credit Services, was appointed Assistant Secretary for Rural Development and Conservation; and a newly created Office of Rural Areas Development,[19] plus the Forest Service, the Soil Conservation Service, and the Farmer Cooperative Service were added to his area of responsibility. Ralph's stabilization functions were given to Duncan, who became Assistant Secretary for Marketing and Stabilization; he also acquired the Extension Service. The Agricultural Research Service and the Cooperative State Experiment Station Service now reported direct to the Secretary and Under Secretary, as did the Foreign Agricultural Service.

The next year Assistant Secretary Duncan resigned, and his agricultural stabilization functions were given to Under Secretary Murphy, whose high organizational level, political experience, and contacts would assure prompt, authoritative handling of any matters that might seem sensitive to Congress. Duncan's successor, Mehren, was named Assistant Secretary for Marketing and Consumer Services. A new assistant secretary, Roland Renne, was placed in charge of foreign agricultural activities.

The next step was the appointment of a Director of Science and Education, Dr. Nyle Brady, a Cornell professor. He was given jurisdiction over the Agricultural Research Service, the Extension Service, and the Cooperative State Experiment Station Service, now renamed the Cooperative State Research Service.

A new major organization, the Consumer and Marketing Service, was created in 1965. This was the old Agricultural Marketing Service, plus meat inspection functions from the Agricultural Research Service, plus warehouse inspection duties from the Agricultural Stabilization and Conservation Service. The objective of this change was to provide more emphasis and more effective organization for consumer protection services and consumer food programs.

[19] Later (February 1965) changed to Rural Community Development Service.

Administrative Organization

Two principal changes in the organization of administrative support services were made by Administrative Assistant Secretary Robertson. One was the creation of an Office of Management Appraisal and Systems Development in lieu of the old Office of Administrative Management, which had been chiefly concerned with directives and organization charts. The other was the establishment of a new Office of Management Services, to do personnel, budget, and other administrative work for organizations too small to sustain their own managerial staffs.

Program and Legislative Developments

As alphabetical agencies of the department were regrouped and renamed, their program purposes were presented by the Secretary under a new alphabet as his "A-B-C-D Program," meaning:

Abundance—Distribution of surplus foods both domestically and abroad; the food stamp plan; school lunches; promotion of good nutrition.
Balance—the price stabilization and production control programs.
Conservation—Soil and water conservation and improved land use planning.
Development—Aid to develop impoverished rural areas.[20]

Secretary Freeman made legislative proposals and program changes on all of these fronts. Like his predecessors, he had the greatest difficulty with measures to control production. He gave probably the greatest public emphasis to rural development. By 1962 the ABCD's had become three C's—Consumers, Communities, and Commodities—but the objectives and the programs were the same.

At the very beginning of Freeman's administration, as noted earlier, he gave priority to legislative efforts to relieve the impending feed grains surplus. A law was enacted in March 1961 under

[20] *Report of the Secretary of Agriculture 1962*, p. 4.

which farmers were paid for diverting corn and sorghum acreage to "conserving" use.[21]

Some Reverses

The following year an attempt to advance in the same direction on a broader front ran into defeat. The administration had proposed a bill providing for rigid acreage controls and guaranteed prices, and Freeman spent many hours discussing its virtues with members of Congress. Said one close observer:

> Few Cabinet members have sought so assiduously to cultivate Senators and Representatives as Freeman has in the 18 months that he has been Secretary . . . [He] says that this person-to-person approach paid off when he was Governor of Minnesota for six years and that he sees no reason why it should not work in Washington.[22]

One reason why it did not work in Washington was that counter-lobbying by the American Farm Bureau Federation prevailed with members of Congress who were in favor of price supports *without* production controls. Freeman had strong White House support—support which did not hesitate to mention patronage and government contracts—but the bill was sent back to committee by a narrow margin. (A bill was later enacted, extending wheat and feed grain controls for a year.)

Another blow rocked the department almost immediately: the Billie Sol Estes case. Estes was a Texas speculator who sold fertilizer, ran a grain storage business, and raised cotton. It was discovered that he had used improper means to acquire federal permits to plant cotton. He had benefited from political aid in Washington and from lax administration at the local level. Before the Estes case was over the Department of Agriculture had been subjected to unfavorable publicity and a Senate investigation. Department officials had been guilty of little malfeasance but much bad judgment, and it was clear that there had to be closer links between Washington policies and local enforcement. As a result regulations were tightened, the Agricultural Stabilization and Conserva-

---

[21] *Report of the Secretary of Agriculture 1961*, p. 57.
[22] Julius Duscha in the *Washington Post*, June 19, 1962.

tion Service was reorganized, and an Office of Inspector General established to do "eye and ear" work for the Secretary.

A third well-publicized reverse came a year later when the country's wheat growers voted against a recommended plan for tighter production controls.

General Program Progress

Freeman lost these battles, but in general his war was going well. In the first three years of his administration net farm income increased by an average of almost $1 billion per year.[23] Price supports had proven effective for wheat, feed grains, and soybeans, although they had not solved cotton growers' income problems.[24] Crop insurance programs were expanded, as were incentives and technical aid to encourage soil conservation practices.

Rural development, a program which the Benson administration had started on a pilot basis and expanded toward the end of its term, was given much more emphasis by Freeman as the Rural Areas Development Program. The Office of Rural Areas Development was started to stimulate and coordinate its progress. Federal agencies both inside and outside the Department of Agriculture (particularly the Area Redevelopment Administration) worked together on programs to provide more education, skills, training, housing, and new industries as attacks on rural poverty. Community committees kept the program pulled together and moving. All of the agencies of the department had a share in the program. One particular policy change from the previous administration was the aggressive expansion of the rural electrification and rural telephone programs.

Other programs too expanded from 1961 to 1964: soil conservation; conversion of cropland to grass or trees; research, reforestation, and recreation in the national forests; and continuing research to improve farm practices. Another successful effort was that to increase agricultural exports. Market studies, tariff negotiations, sales promotion efforts, and the Food-for-Peace Program

[23] *Department of Agriculture Appropriations for 1965*, Hearings before a subcommittee of the House Appropriations Committee, 88 Cong. 2 sess. (1964), p. 7.
[24] *Report of the Secretary of Agriculture 1963*, pp. 20–22.

helped achieve a record export level of $5.1 billion in fiscal years 1962 and 1963.[25]

Domestic surplus food donation programs also continued to expand. One program change was reminiscent of the New Deal: a food stamp plan, started in eight pilot areas in 1962 and expanded to thirty-three in 1963.[26]

By and large the structure and the staff of the department proved adaptable to these program moves. Officials who had served under Presidents Franklin Roosevelt and Harry Truman welcomed Freeman's policies as a return to earlier objectives after what one of them called "a period of military occupation." It was hard, of course, for some of the bureaucrats to get "turned around." One of the Freeman team told the author of several instances in which new orders by the Secretary were not carried out by one of the larger services until there had been repeated emphatic follow-ups, but on the whole, the machinery worked well.

Policies and Budgets Under a New President

When officials of the Department of Agriculture were asked about the impact of President Johnson's taking over, their answers were like those heard in the other departments in this study: "No real policy changes, but he certainly means business on economy." Agriculture's budget, like Interior's, climbed rapidly to support the program expansions, but then leveled off in 1964. Unlike Interior's, it was to go down in 1965 and 1966.[27]

Fiscal Year	Actual Expenditures (in millions)
1961	$5,929
1962	6,669
1963	7,735
1964	7,897
1965	6,975 (enacted)
1966	6,357 (est.)

[25] *Department of Agriculture Appropriations for 1965*, Hearings, p. 336.

[26] *Report of the Secretary of Agriculture 1963*, p. 39.

[27] Source: *The Budget of the United States Government* for the fiscal years concerned.

Within three weeks of his reelection President Johnson announced, through Secretary Freeman, that present farm policies would continue, with no major changes or new control programs.[28] This was soon followed, however, by two unofficial but significant statements that looked like handwriting on the wall. The first was a speech by Willard Cochrane, who had left the department as Director of Agricultural Economics in July 1964. Cochrane said in effect that urban voters would tire of supporting farm subsidies and that sharp curtailment of federal supports could be expected in three to ten years.[29] The next voice was that of Kermit Gordon, Director of the Bureau of the Budget, who pointed out that federal price supports went mainly to the one million most prosperous farmers who need federal aid the least. He said that the 2.5 million small farmers cannot be expected to operate successful commercial farms and that "they require assistance in the painful transition to nonfarm jobs . . ."[30] There was an immediate outcry by the farm bloc leaders in Congress.

The President's farm message in February 1965 avoided controversy by recommending no new controls or subsidies. It did propose a long-range program to take more land out of production. The President said he would set up a commission to examine the nation's entire agricultural policy.[31] He unquestionably needed some sort of help in his dilemma. He was insisting on severe economies in order to finance new programs of the Great Society while keeping the 1966 federal budget under $100 billion. Meanwhile, about half of the Agriculture budget was going to price supports which seemed likely to escalate unless politically unpopular reductions were imposed. The legislative branch was also uncooperative on one specific Johnson economy, the closing of twenty small farm research stations at an estimated saving of $5 million.[32] This was postponed under congressional pressure but later accomplished for the most part. And all the while agricultural produc-

[28] Washington Post, Nov. 22, 1964.

[29] Washington Post, Dec. 30, 1964.

[30] Kermit Gordon, "How Much Should Government Do?" Saturday Review, Vol. 48 (Jan. 9, 1965), p. 27.

[31] Washington Post, Feb. 5, 1965.

[32] New York Times, Feb. 4, 1965.

tivity continued to rise, increasing the likelihood of a policy crisis in the future. A new and difficult aspect was posed by a report of the Commission on Civil Rights finding racial discrimination in the administration of Department of Agriculture programs.[33]

These problems would have to be faced without the help of Under Secretary Murphy, who was named to head the Civil Aeronautics Board in 1965. Continuity was assured, however, by the promotion of Schnittker, the top economist, to Under Secretary.

A Strong Change of Command

The Department of Agriculture, like its older and smaller sister, Interior, was taken over by an alert, knowledgeable young Secretary who provided strong program leadership and devoted much effort to his legislative program. He established new directions in policy, notably stronger efforts to limit production, and a total attack on rural poverty, and chose his men and organized his agencies to increase his chances of success. He was less successful than Udall in getting his total program through Congress. In general, however, he took charge effectively, and his administration was one of vitality and development.

[33] *Washington Post*, March 1, 1965.

HEALTH, EDUCATION, AND WELFARE

New Programs, Shifting Leadership

. . . we will do what must be done. For our national
household is cluttered with unfinished and neglected tasks.

—President Kennedy
State of the Union Message,
January 29, 1961

LIKE INTERIOR and Agriculture, the De-
partment of Health, Education, and Welfare went through a
period of change and expansion from 1961 to 1964, but it did so
under different leadership circumstances. While Secretaries Udall
and Freeman were pressing vigorously over the full four-year
period for new legislation and expanded programs, Health, Education, and Welfare had two secretaries and responded to various
other sources of direction. Abraham Ribicoff and Anthony J.
Celebrezze made important contributions, but much of the motive
power came from elsewhere: the White House, Congress, the
operating agencies of the department, and Assistant Secretary
(for Legislation) Wilbur J. Cohen.

Other contrasts with Interior and Agriculture were less sharp.
There were a few changes in the HEW top staff during the four
years, and one major change in organization: the creation of the
Welfare Administration.

The Starting Team

The new group that took over the department in 1961 was a mixture of politicians and professionals. The new Secretary, like those at Interior and Agriculture, was a personable and aggressive politician. Abraham Ribicoff, a Connecticut lawyer, had served two terms in Congress and was in his second term as governor of his state. He had been an early and vigorous supporter of Kennedy in the 1960 campaigns. The Under Secretary picked for, rather than by, Ribicoff was Ivan A. Nestingen, mayor of Madison, Wisconsin, another timely rooter for JFK. A defeated congressman from Pennsylvania, James M. Quigley, was chosen for Assistant Secretary, a job with no specified responsibilities. Quigley became coordinator of action on two of the department's more difficult problems, civil rights and water pollution control.

The other assistant secretaryship, the department's top legislative job, was filled by an "old pro", Wilbur J. Cohen, who had been chief researcher for the Social Security Administration in the Truman administration and professor of public welfare administration at the University of Michigan during the latter Eisenhower years. Cohen had headed the President-elect's task force on health and social security. Another well-informed returnee was General Counsel Alanson W. Willcox, who came back to virtually the same post he had held in 1951. The position of Administrative Assistant Secretary, created at the very end of the Eisenhower administration, was filled by a career administrator, Rufus E. Miles, Jr., who had been filling essentially the same job for the preceding eight years. Before that he had served in top administrative and policy positions in the old Federal Security Agency, HEW's predecessor.

Two top health officials were chosen with the active help of Senator Lister Hill of Alabama, chairman of the Senate Committee on Labor and Public Welfare. The new Surgeon General of the Public Health Service was Dr. Luther L. Terry, who had been Assistant Director of the National Heart Institute.[1] The position

---

[1] By law, the Surgeon General is appointed by the President from the Commissioned Corps of the Public Health Service for a four-year term. Dr. Terry's predecessor, Dr. Leroy E. Burney, was nominated in August 1956 but not confirmed by

of Special Assistant to the Secretary (Health and Medical Affairs) —a job equivalent to assistant secretary—was filled for the first time by a non-physician. The choice was Boisfeuillet Jones, administrator of health services of Emory University.

Among the top jobs the most difficult to fill was that of Commissioner of Education. Press reports said that it had been offered unsuccessfully to a variety of top educators.[2] Some of those approached expressed doubt that the position had the stature to influence educational policy; some were apprehensive about its political vulnerability; some simply preferred to stay where they were. The search ended soon after inauguration with the appointment of Sterling M. McMurrin, academic vice president and professor of philosophy at the University of Utah, a well-regarded educator.

The heads of the other four operating agencies of the department were long-service professionals who simply stayed on: William L. Mitchell, Commissioner of Social Security; George P. Larrick, Commissioner of Food and Drugs; Mary E. Switzer, Director of Vocational Rehabilitation; and Dr. Winfred Overholser, Superintendent of Saint Elizabeths Hospital.

Taking Over From the Republicans

The actual transition process in HEW was carried on with care and goodwill. Secretary Ribicoff was the first cabinet officer named. His appointment was announced on December 1, 1960, and he showed up at the department five days later to meet with outgoing Secretary Arthur S. Flemming and with Rufus Miles, who then had the title of Director of Administration. Appearing at a joint press conference with Flemming, Ribicoff announced that his main legislative concerns would be health care for the aged and federal aid to education.

Both Flemming and Miles were intent on easing the transfer

---

the Senate until early 1957. Thus his term ran out at the change of administration —a factor tending to open the choice to political influences more than might otherwise have been the case.

[2] *Evening Star* (Washington), Jan. 11, 1961; *Washington Post,* Jan. 26, 1961.

of power. Flemming was a conscientious administrator who had held high federal posts almost continuously since 1939. Apart from Miles's natural interest in smoothing the path of his new boss, he had become an expert in the orientation of new political executives. He had made a study of this subject under a Rockefeller Public Service Award and had published two articles on it.[3] Briefing material had already been prepared under Miles's direction, but Ribicoff was still too busy with his gubernatorial responsibilities to deal with it. He was mailed a packet of legislative and program material on December 21, and Miles and Reginald Conley, the Assistant General Counsel in charge of legislation, went to Hartford for two days to discuss it with him.

Ribicoff returned to the department on December 28 for a day of meetings with the heads of the operating agencies. He held another press conference, mainly to announce that he was discussing the department's legislative aims in great detail. He said that he would keep on "many" of the career staff and that he would promote Miles to Administrative Assistant Secretary if he had not been so promoted by January 20, 1961.[4] (The promotion did take place before then.)

Meanwhile Flemming and his staff were preparing voluminous legislative recommendations which were all sent to "the Hill" before inauguration. These were an effort neither to commit nor to embarrass the incoming administration but rather to tidy things up, to take advantage of the staff work that had been done, and possibly to provide a focus for a liberal Republican position in Congress.[5] Further briefing material was given to Ribicoff, including biographical information about key officials. The new staff reported that they found this material useful.

The new Surgeon General, Dr. Terry, although a veteran Public

[3] Rufus E. Miles, Jr., "The Orientation of Presidential Appointees", *Public Administration Review*, Vol. 18 (Winter 1958), pp. 1-6; and "The Orientation of Presidential Appointees: A Continuing Challenge", *Public Administration Review*, Vol. 18 (Spring 1958), pp. 106-12.

[4] *Washington Post*, Dec. 29, 1960.

[5] One high career official, referring to Secretary Flemming's enthusiastic tendency, even at this late date, to overload his work schedule, remarked, "Arthur has to be out of here by noon on January 20, and at the rate he's going he'll never make it." And he didn't; he was still cleaning out papers the next day.

Health Service officer, had had no experience in the top administration of the service, and so found it helpful to work side-by-side with Dr. Burney for a few days before inauguration.

Program Commitments and Guidance

No department head covered in this study—indeed, none in the government—had his program objectives more clearly and emphatically outlined for him in advance than did Secretary Ribicoff. The Democratic platform and President Kennedy's campaign statements committed the new administration to Social Security-financed health insurance for the aged; increased resources for medical facilities, instruction, and research; greater federal support for all levels of education; and to many related purposes.

These aims became much more explicit in early January 1961 when the reports of two Kennedy task forces were released. First to be made public was the report on education, released January 6. The task force, headed by President Frederick Hovde of Purdue University,[6] recommended direct federal support of public school operating budgets; grants and loans for housing and academic facilities; and broadening of the National Defense Education Act, particularly to benefit teachers at all levels.[7]

Four days later the task force report on health and welfare was made public. This group was chaired by Assistant Secretary-to-be Cohen.[8] The most publicized recommendation was for medical care benefits for older persons financed through the Social Security system. Other health proposals in the report included: aid to medical schools (and other institutions training health personnel)

[6] Other members were Russell Thackrey, executive secretary of the Land Grant Colleges Association; Benjamin Willis, Chicago Superintendent of Schools; Alvin Eurich, vice president of the Ford Foundation; and John Gardner, president of the Carnegie Corporation.

[7] For the complete text see "6. Educational Frontiers" in *New Frontiers of the Kennedy Administration* (Public Affairs Press, 1961), pp. 65–69.

[8] Other members: Dean A. Clark, professor at Harvard Medical School; Robert E. Cooke, professor at Johns Hopkins School of Medicine; James Dixon, president of Antioch College; Joshua Lederburg, professor at Stanford School of Medicine; Herman M. Somers, professor of political science at Haverford College; and Elizabeth Wickenden, public welfare consultant.

through partial subsidies of operating costs, construction grants, and scholarship grants; continued federal support of medical research; expansion of the Hill-Burton medical facilities program; establishment of a National Academy of Health; and creation of a National Institute of Child Health.

There were also some public welfare recommendations: aid to children of an unemployed parent; an integrated "Family and Child Welfare Services Plan," which would bring together in one program legislation for aid to needy families and children; and aid for community social services. Finally, it was urged that the Children's Bureau be made a staff agency in the Office of the Secretary, with its health grants being transferred to the Public Health Service and its child welfare services program moving to the Social Security Administration.[9]

Program and Legislative Developments

The first flurry of activity for the new Secretary was not concerned with changes in major programs but with specific activities in one problem area: help to the Cuban refugees in Miami. The Eisenhower administration had established relief and assistance activities there for these people. Ribicoff flew to Miami a few days after inauguration to look over the situation, to promise continuing help to the Cubans, and to coordinate future aid by all the federal departments concerned.[10] President Kennedy, on Ribicoff's recommendation, then announced a $4 million program of assistance: health, relief, resettlement, food distribution, and employment.[11]

Another early development in the department was characteristic of the Kennedy administration. The touch-football-playing President and Attorney General reinvigorated the President's Council on Youth Fitness, moved it from Interior to Health, Education, and Welfare, and brought in a big-name athletic figure, University

---

[9] For the complete text see *Congressional Record*, Vol. 107, Pt. 1, 87 Cong. 1 sess. (1961), pp. 728–30.

[10] *New York Times*, Jan. 27 and 30, 1961.

[11] *New York Times*, Feb. 4, 1961.

of Oklahoma football coach "Bud" Wilkinson, to provide leadership.

Welfare

Much of Ribicoff's own energy during his year-and-a-half tenure as Secretary went into public relations and congressional relations efforts on behalf of improved welfare legislation. He soon obtained a temporary law authorizing for the first time aid to dependent children whose parents are unemployed.[12] By the end of 1961 a special committee he had appointed recommended substantial program changes, with emphasis on rehabilitation of relief clients.[13] Two months later President Kennedy sent an emphatic and comprehensive package of recommendations to Congress, stressing preventive and rehabilitative services; aid to entire families; more realistic eligibility requirements; increased training of personnel; more research and demonstration projects; and increased aid to states that bring together administration of their relief programs for the aged, blind, and disabled with medical assistance programs for the aged.[14] The message was largely consistent with the report of Cohen's pre-inaugural task force. A new law based on the message was on the books by the end of July—thanks partly to Ribicoff's efforts and partly to widespread public realization of the need for welfare reforms.

"Medicare"

Less success attended the Kennedy administration's efforts to enact a plan of medical aid for the aged financed through Social Security. For some ten years battle lines on this issue had been clearly drawn between political parties and between clientele groups. The proposal was a lineal descendant of President Truman's recommendations for government-financed comprehensive

[12] U. S. Department of Health, Education, and Welfare, *Annual Report 1961*, p. 8.
[13] *Washington Post*, Dec. 5, 1961.
[14] *New York Times*, Feb. 2, 1962.

health insurance. "Medicare," as the plan came to be known, was supported by liberal Democrats and organized labor, and opposed by most Republicans, conservative Democrats, and organized medicine. It was highlighted as a campaign issue after Congress failed to enact it following the party conventions of 1960.

President Kennedy formally proposed "medicare" to Congress less than three weeks after his inauguration, and opposition immediately developed. Probably the key factor was the reluctance of Chairman Wilbur Mills of the House Committee on Ways and Means to support the bill. The administration and labor lobbyists continued to press for such legislation from year to year, and President Johnson again recommended it in a broad health message to Congress early in 1964,[15] but Congress did not act. Following the strong Democratic triumph in the 1964 elections, however, the measure had smooth sailing, and it was enacted in the summer of 1965.

Meanwhile other federal health activities made progress. Support of medical research continued at high levels, and there were new and expanded programs in the fields of environmental health and community health. Two important new health laws went into effect in the autumn of 1963. One authorized construction grants and student loan funds in medical schools and other facilities for the health professions.[16] The other, resulting partly from the strong interest of President Kennedy in dealing with mental retardation, provided grants to construct research and treatment centers for the mentally retarded and community mental health centers.[17]

Another health matter that resulted in headlines for one of the department's programs concerned new drugs. Sleeping pills containing a substance called thalidomide had been held off the market by order of Dr. Frances Kelsey, a Food and Drug official, because of lack of evidence as to their safety. Several cases in Europe showed that when pregnant women took the pills their babies might turn out to be horribly deformed. The incident made

[15] *Washington Post,* Feb. 11, 1964.
[16] U. S. Library of Congress, Legislative Reference Service, *Enactments by the 88th Congress Concerning Education and Training 1963–1964,* pp. 9–18.
[17] *Ibid.,* pp. 18–36.

a heroine of Dr. Kelsey and helped in the enactment in 1962 of the Kefauver-Harris Drug Amendments. The new provisions, long sought by the department, gave authority for more effective investigation of the safety and adequacy of new drugs.

Aid to Education

Education legislation, another priority matter for Ribicoff, Cohen, and the White House staff, took up untold hours of staff time, testimony, and—on Capitol Hill—controversy in 1961, 1962, and 1963. The results, an impressive collection of measures, were approved by President Johnson within his first month in office. They included: a $1.2 billion authorization for construction of higher education facilities; increased grants for vocational education; broadening of the National Defense Education Act; extension of "federally impacted areas" legislation; and the occupational counseling and schooling provisions in amendments to the Manpower Development and Training Act.[18]

Meanwhile direct aid to elementary and secondary schools was held up because of controversy over the church-state implications of government funds being granted to (or withheld from) religious schools. Early in 1965 President Johnson offered a novel and sweeping proposal: $1.5 billion of aid, primarily for children of low-income families. Direct aid to parochial schools was avoided, but their pupils could take some courses at public schools under shared time or dual enrollment arrangements.[19]

Leadership in the Department

These legislative developments, particularly those concerning welfare and education, were Secretary Ribicoff's main concern during his early months in office. It was a more complex legislative concern than that faced by other department heads because of the number of Senate and House committees with jurisdiction over HEW matters. The Secretary must answer to both

[18] *Ibid.*, pp. 36–82.
[19] *Washington Post,* Jan. 13, 1965.

Commerce committees, Ways and Means (House), Finance (Senate), Labor and Public Welfare (Senate), Education and Labor (House), both Government Operations committees, and even both Agriculture committees. Such an assignment would be a severe test of any department head, even if he had no administrative responsibilities.

Ribicoff, like most of the department heads discussed in this book, was little concerned with administration. Top officials of the operating agencies found him difficult to communicate with, particularly as compared with Flemming, who was much given to staff papers and extensive group discussions. The new Secretary made many of his decisions in consultation only with Assistant Secretary Cohen and with his "outer office" executive assistant Jon Newman, a young Hartford lawyer. Cohen's professional knowledge and experience and his willingness to pour extraordinary amounts of time and energy into his work soon made him the central figure on policy and legislative matters. He dealt with presidential assistants Theodore Sorensen, Myer Feldman, and others on the White House staff, and on occasion with the President himself on legislative strategy and content.

Meanwhile it had become apparent to the department's officials that Ribicoff was losing interest in his job, and his resignation in mid-1962 to run for United States Senator from Connecticut was no surprise. He had commented that the department was too large and complex to administer, and he had found less satisfaction in legislative activity downtown than he had on the Hill.[20]

Various rumors about the identity of Ribicoff's successor proved untrue, and there was general surprise when the President named Anthony J. Celebrezze, a popular Cleveland politician and lawyer who had been elected mayor of his city five times. Celebrezze soon established warm relationships with officials throughout the department and began a quiet style of administration. One veteran executive remarked that Ribicoff kept looking for opportunities to make political impact, but that Celebrezze thought it a good day if no criticism was made or notice taken of the department.

[20] *Washington Post*, July 13 and 22, 1962.

Other '62 Turnover

There were other important personnel changes in 1962. In fact, new heads were named for three of the department's six operating agencies. All three changes, in the judgment of the Secretary's staff and of other close observers, tended to strengthen the department.

William L. Mitchell retired as Commissioner of Society Security after some forty years of government service. Ribicoff appointed another veteran career employee to succeed him: Robert M. Ball, Deputy Director of the Bureau of Old-Age and Survivors Insurance and a Rockefeller Public Service Award winner.

Next to depart was Commissioner of Education McMurrin, who resigned to go back to the University of Utah. McMurrin again raised the issue of stature and influence of the Commissioner's job. He deplored its low organizational status, the slowness of its bureaucracy, and the reluctance of Congress to provide resources.[21] He also complained about the conservatism and power of leaders in professional education organizations. McMurrin's successor, named after a two-month gap, was a widely applauded choice, Dean Francis Keppel of the Faculty of Education at Harvard. Newspaper accounts of his appointment hinted that he had assurance of White House backing in changes he might institute in the Office of Education,[22] and the President was significantly present when Keppel took the oath of office.

About the same time Dr. Winfred Overholser completed a quarter of a century as Superintendent of St. Elizabeths Hospital and reached mandatory retirement age. Dr. Dale Cameron, a commissioned Public Health Service officer who had been understudying him for about a year, stepped into the job. Cameron had made a career of management of mental health institutions.

Other Personnel Effects

These changes were neither unusual nor attributable to the change of administration. Changes at lower levels were negligible.

[21] *New York Times,* July 28 and Sept. 9, 1962, and *Washington Post,* Nov. 4, 1962.
[22] *New York Times,* Nov. 25, 1962.

A few of Secretary Flemming's assistants left and were replaced, but otherwise there was no general turnover of either "Schedule C" or career employees. Cohen did expand his staff in order to carry out the heavy legislative program. As time went on special assistants to the Under Secretary were added for such new functions as manpower development and educational television. Otherwise the career staffs carried on with both old and new program activities.

Two personnel developments in the Public Health Service came to public attention in the already busy year of 1962. One involved a series of charges of unethical activity against supervisory officials made by disgruntled Washington employees.[23] The Secretary's office appointed an impartial investigative team to look into the problems, a few supervisory personnel were shifted, and the matter died down.

Much more significant was the release of the report of a distinguished committee headed by former Secretary Marion B. Folsom which made a seven-month study of Public Health Service personnel systems. The report urged better leadership, coordination, and organization of both the Commissioned Corps and civil service personnel systems, forecasts of manpower needs, continuous recruiting, a career development program, and increased pay.[24] The service started action promptly to put the recommendations into effect.[25]

Early in 1965 Under Secretary Nestingen resigned following reports of disputes with Cohen, and the latter was promoted to take his place.

The Organization

The Department of Health, Education, and Welfare is such a sprawling and diverse assembly of agencies and subagencies that the unitary term "department" seems ironic. The various operat-

[23] *Washington Post,* March 2, 1962.

[24] *Report of the Advisory Committee on Public Health Service Personnel Systems* (U. S. Department of Health, Education, and Welfare, March 1962).

[25] U. S. Department of Health, Education, and Welfare, *Annual Report 1963,* p. 130.

ing agencies (and indeed certain of the bureaus and divisions of the larger agencies) have widely differing histories, constituencies, and functions. Nevertheless, it is legally a department, headed by one man reporting to the President. Its various secretaries have kept final control of the department's budget, legislative program, and the most important public relations and administrative matters, but most of them have had only a modest influence over policy development and coordination. The sheer size and diversity of the department is part of the problem (although the Department of Defense story—Chapter 3—suggests that large diverse departments *can* be managed by a Secretary). A more formidable problem is the attitude of Congress, which has kept the size of the Secretary's staff at levels too low to allow real *management* of the department by the Secretary.

When Secretary Ribicoff resigned he said the task was impossible, noting that with 112 operating programs, more than 70,000 employees, and a $4 billion budget, HEW is too cumbersome to be administered properly. In Ribicoff's judgment, HEW should be split into three departments.[26] His predecessor, Secretary Flemming, was not of the same opinion. He maintained that the department was a viable organization. Yet he had neither the time (he served less than two and a half years) nor the resources to make lasting progress in analysis and integration of program policies across agency lines.

Despite these difficulties no practical alternatives to HEW's makeup were advanced, although rumors were circulating in 1965 that President Johnson would make the Office of Education and the National Science Foundation into a new "Department of Education."[27] Meanwhile the confederation stayed loose.

The Welfare Administration

The major organization change made during the Kennedy administration was the creation of the Welfare Administration in

26 *Washington Post,* July 22, 1962.

27 For an earlier summary of the principal issues involved in such a proposal, see George W. Oakes, "Chances for a Department of Education," *Sunday Star* (Washington), May 6, 1962.

January 1963. After Robert Ball became Commissioner of the Social Security Administration he found himself turning from one large full-time job (head of the nationwide social insurance organization) to another (head of all welfare activities). Both seemed to him too large and too important to be submerged organizationally. Assistant Secretaries Cohen and Miles joined Ball in convincing Secretary Celebrezze that the Bureau of Family Services and the Children's Bureau should be merged into a new Welfare Administration.[28] The plan went into effect after Cohen recruited Ellen Winston, Commissioner of Welfare of North Carolina, as the first head of the new organization. Mrs. Winston was a strong advocate of the preventive, protective, rehabilitative approach to welfare administration favored on the New Frontier.[29] This organizational decision partially put into effect the administrative recommendations of Cohen's pre-inaugural task force, but did not take the further, politically riskier, step of dismembering the Children's Bureau.[30]

Lesser Changes

There were a number of internal structural changes made in the operating agencies to help them meet new program demands. Early in 1961, for example, President Kennedy announced the establishment of a new Child Health Center at the National Institutes of Health, Public Health Service. Two years later legislation made this Center, plus the Center for Aging Research and the Division of General Medical Sciences, into a new National Institute of Child Health and Human Development. (A "National Institute of Child Health" had been recommended by the Cohen task force.)

In the Office of Education, perpetually plagued by internal administrative problems, an organization study had been started before the change of administration. Commissioner McMurrin encouraged its completion, and the basic recommendations were put into effect in the spring of 1962. They provided for a better inte-

---

[28] The Bureau of Federal Credit Unions remained with Social Security.

[29] *Washington Post*, Dec. 20, 1962.

[30] See above, p. 102.

grated organization consisting of three main bureaus (Educational Research and Development, Educational Assistance Programs, and International Education) plus an Office of Legislative and Program Planning. The change had been delayed for months because a recommendation for establishment of an educational policy center had come under fire from congressional critics who saw it as a move toward federal control of education,[31] and the center was dropped. After Keppel became Commissioner a Bureau of Higher Education Facilities was added to the structure.[32]

Organization changes were also made in the Food and Drug Administration in 1963, many of them developing from recommendations of a Citizens Advisory Committee the previous year. A new Bureau of Education and Voluntary Compliance was set up to achieve both more emphasis upon and more coordination of consumer education and industry education programs. At the same time other changes were made to upgrade FDA's scientific work and its planning activities.

Another 1963 change affected nomenclature more than organization: the Office of Vocational Rehabilitation became the Vocational Rehabilitation Administration and its Director became a Commissioner, a more prestigious title in the department.

There was no significant change in the organization of the Office of the Secretary, but four events deserve mention. First, legislation was requested early in 1961 to authorize a third assistant secretary. Ribicoff intended to use this official to coordinate the department's growing international responsibilities—educational exchanges, work with the Agency for International Development, research grants abroad, and so on. Congress did not authorize the position, and the function remained an inconspicuous part of Assistant Secretary Quigley's responsibilities. Second, a new operations analysis staff was established under the Comptroller to do depth studies of program management problems. Third, the Special Staff on Aging, a point of coordination for programs affecting "senior citizens," was moved from the Office of the Secretary to the new Welfare Administration and renamed the Office of Aging.

---

[31] *Washington Post*, March 1, 1962.
[32] In 1965 the office was facing yet another reorganization.

Fourth, an Office of Juvenile Delinquency was also moved to the Welfare Administration.

The Wherewithal

For those who like to use dollars to keep score, the Department of Health, Education, and Welfare had the most impressive growth of any of the departments discussed in this book. Expenditures rose steadily, went through a Johnsonian economy sag in 1965, and seemed ready for a big jump in 1966: [33]

Fiscal Year	Actual Expenditures (in millions)
1961	$3,685
1962	4,215
1963	4,909
1964	5,498
1965	5,356 (enacted)
1966	7,776 (est.)

Virtually all programs expanded, with the largest increases going to welfare grants, education, community mental health, environmental health, medical research of all kinds, and expansion of the Food and Drug Administration.

White House Relations: New Frontier and Great Society

The White House was deeply involved in the formulation and handling of the department's legislative proposals on welfare, aid to education, and "medicare." Assistant Secretary Cohen worked closely with President Kennedy's staff on these measures.

When Lyndon Johnson became President there was no substantive change in policy at first—just economy measures of the sort already mentioned for other departments. White House contacts declined in frequency as President Johnson showed an inclination to give department heads more freedom in policy devel-

---

[33] Source: *The Budget of the United States Government* for the fiscal years concerned. Expenditures do not include Social Security Trust Fund expenditures.

opment than President Kennedy had. The advent of the Johnson "Great Society" program, however, caused an upsurge in White House contacts. Health, Education, and Welfare officials became intricately involved in plans for the Economic Opportunity and Appalachia programs, as well as in the apparently never-ending work on "medicare" and aid to education.

Interpreting the Progress

The observer wonders how the Department of Health, Education, and Welfare got through such a dynamic and demanding period with so little visible leadership. Much new legislation was passed; programs increased in size and variety; finances doubled; a major organization change took place; and half of the agency heads were replaced. Yet Secretary Ribicoff served only a year and a half and supplied only modest leadership toward the end of that period. Secretary Celebrezze, in contrast to all of his predecessors, was a neophyte among the complexities of top-level wheeling and dealing in Washington. Who, then, held the department together and kept it moving? There are several answers. The professionals in the operating agencies and the career staff in the Office of the Secretary both contributed a mixture of progress and stability. The operating agency heads, both new and old, were almost all top "pros" in their fields. The chairmen and staff members of the congressional committees most concerned were familiar with the department's programs. And finally, the same sort of energizing effect that was produced in Defense, Interior, and Agriculture by new department heads and by the President himself at State came from Assistant Secretary Cohen. As in the other departments, the transition had been a story of both problems and progress.

Yet the most favorable factors in the Department of Health, Education, and Welfare's progress were human needs and the temper of the times. The voting public and their congressmen were ready for much more federal activity in all three of the department's concerns. The Kennedy and Johnson administrations released the brakes, but they cannot take full credit for furnishing motive power.

7 / THE FEDERAL AVIATION AGENCY
New Techniques and Relationships

> We seek an integrated national aviation program within
> a broad national transportation policy which will make a
> maximum contribution to economic growth, national secur-
> ity, cultural advancement, and international trade and
> commerce.
>
> —President Kennedy
> Letter to Administrator, Federal
> Aviation Agency, September 6, 1961

THE SAME December 1960 newspapers that
told of preparations for the Kennedy administration also showed
pictures of the debris from a catastrophic collision between two
airliners near New York City. This disaster drew renewed attention to the rules, the equipment, and the people who regulate air
travel—in short, to the Federal Aviation Agency. Some observers
recalled that a similar crash over the Grand Canyon in 1956 was
one of the factors that led to the establishment of the FAA in 1958.

There was deep public concern over the 1960 accident and
others, although there had been no increase in accident rates.
there were such sharp increases both in use of aircraft and in
cern of any informed observer (as, for example, an incoming President) over the sheer manageability of air traffic at a time when
there were such sharp increases both in use of aircraft and in
aircraft performance. Another was the concern of airline pilots,
airplane owners, and the whole air transportation industry over
relationships with the Federal Aviation Agency. Their attitude

developed naturally from the fact that this nearly new agency had more authority than its predecessor, the Civil Aeronautics Administration, and from the belief that its first Administrator, General E. R. Quesada, had handled them roughly.

The General, an old-time Army Air Force pilot, was almost a military stereotype in his blunt decisiveness. He had administered the agency forcefully and with great dedication to the public interest as he saw it—an approach that had won him more respect than liking from the aviation industry.

Thus public concern, the need for technological advances, and the question of relationships added up to an interesting bundle of problems waiting for the incoming administration.[1]

Starting Out the New Administrator

And wait they did, for Najeeb E. Halaby, the new Administrator, was one of the later arrivals on the New Frontier. He was named on January 19, confirmed by the Senate on February 24, and took the oath of office on March 3, 1961. Halaby's qualifications seemed ideal. He was an experienced flight instructor (Army Air Corps), test pilot (Lockheed), lawyer (head of his own firm in Los Angeles), official of a technical research organization (Aerospace Corporation), federal official (Deputy Assistant Secretary of Defense for International Security Affairs), and pro-Kennedy politician. He was on first-name terms with the new President, who announced that he had confidence in Halaby and that there would be no layers of government between them.[2]

Halaby, who had been put on the payroll as a consultant, used the six weeks before he took over to familiarize himself with the operations and problems of the agency. He held no staff meetings and made no decisions but read reams of material and consulted many of the key staff. He was already acquainted with the

---

[1] The outgoing Administrator had problems, too, but they were very different, and less important. He became head of the Washington Senators baseball organization, whose team soon assumed that position in the American League from which advancement opportunities were most extensive.

[2] *Evening Star* (Washington), Jan. 19, 1961.

agency's work and with some of the staff because he had served on the "Harding Committee," a 1955 citizen study group that made recommendations on air safety and air traffic control. Meanwhile "business as usual" was possible because James T. Pyle, Deputy Administrator under Quesada and previously Civil Aeronautics Administrator, was in charge, and there had been virtually no turnover in the top staff.

Preparations for the transition had been going on since November 1960 under the leadership of Alan L. Dean, Assistant Administrator for Management Services. Dean had been the staff member of the Bureau of the Budget who worked on the establishment of the Federal Aviation Agency and had been "Mr. Management" in the agency ever since. Quesada signed a directive naming Dean as transition coordinator and ordering the bureau and division heads to cooperate in preparing for an orderly transfer of responsibility. They were ready to work with a designated representative of the President-elect, but Kennedy never appointed one for FAA.

Six weeks' work then went into preparation of briefing material for the new Administrator. This included documents covering:

The character and scope of FAA
Procedures for internal policy making
The agency budget (fiscal year 1962)
The legislative program
Current problems
Twenty indicators of agency progress
Photographs and descriptions of top staff
Extent and nature of participation by the
    military in the agency

Also included was the Annual Report for the previous year, and a copy of the "Curtis report" recommending the creation of the Federal Aviation Agency.

In addition to his reading during this period, Halaby talked to many of the key staff, not only to learn about their work, but to ask for their suggestions and to get some idea of their capacities. He made a good impression on them in these interviews both because of his knowledge of aviation and because of his analytical attitude in discussing problems.

Task Forces and Technical Advances

Analysis of the agency's mission and operations and planning of its future were the order of the day. President Kennedy had directed Halaby "to chart with precision where U. S. aviation was and where it was headed, but more important, to lay out the course it must take to maintain world leadership."[3] As the charting began, the agency was neither helped nor handicapped by previous commitments. There had been no memorable campaign declarations on aviation policy, and no pre-inaugural task forces had been used. The only statement on the subject in the Democratic platform called for reversal of the Republican policy of " 'an orderly withdrawal' from the airport grant programs" and expansion of the grants instead.[4] Thus the Administrator had considerable freedom to plan his course of action.

"Horizon" and "Beacon"

Halaby promptly launched two important analytical studies to provide guidance for agency policies: Project Horizon, to develop a statement of national aviation goals; and Project Beacon, to plan the safe and efficient utilization of airspace. Both were started in March 1961 at President Kennedy's formal request; both were conducted by task forces of eminent and qualified citizens; and both reported about six months later.

The Project Horizon report[5] recommended some ambitious and varied plans, including more low-fare experiments, at least five new major airports, development of a supersonic air transport

[3] Federal Aviation Agency, *Third Annual Report* (1961) p. vii.
[4] "Complete Text of 1960 Democratic Platform," *Congressional Quarterly Weekly Report*, Vol. 18 (July 15, 1960), p. 1245.
[5] Federal Aviation Agency, *Report of the Task Force on National Aviation Goals* (1961). The task force consisted of Fred M. Glass (chairman), Hertz Corporation; Stanley Gewirtz (vice chairman), formerly of Western Air Lines; Selig Altschul, Aviation Advisory Service; Leslie A. Bryan, University of Illinois; Gerald A. Busch, Lockheed Aircraft Corporation; Francis T. Fox, Los Angeles Department of Airports; John F. Loosbrock, *Air Force Magazine;* and Paul Reiber, formerly of Air Transport Association.

plane, a "massive attack" on aircraft noise, revision of international air route agreements, and many others.[6]

The report on Project Beacon [7] recommended a radically revised system of air traffic control—a single national aviation system, including subsystems on weather, communications, airspace utilization, and airports. A key point in the recommendations was to be use of automatic radio transmitters (called beacons) in airplanes. On receiving the report, President Kennedy ordered an immediate start on putting the recommendations into effect. FAA organized an internal System Design Team and an external Technical Advisory Board to "ride herd" on the necessary developments. Meanwhile, however, an internal report [8] differed with many of Beacon's detailed recommendations, although endorsing its basic concepts and philosophy.

Other Studies

Another important task force also reported in November 1961. This was a special study group of eminent lawyers (Project Tightrope) that had reviewed the agency's rule-making and enforcement procedures. Their report found much to commend, but noted some deficiencies that resulted from a natural sense of urgency and from "evolution too fast to be orderly." [9] Halaby promptly organized a Regulatory Council in his own office to coordinate rule-making and made a number of procedural changes to meet the Tightrope criticisms.[10]

---

[6] *New York Times,* Sept. 10, 1961.

[7] Federal Aviation Agency, *Report of the Task Force on Air Traffic Control* (1961). The task force consisted of Richard R. Hough (chairman), Ohio Bell Telephone Co.; Col. Louis E. Andre, Jr., U. S. Air Force; Harry B. Combs, Combs Aircraft Co.; George C. Comstock, Airborne Instruments Laboratory; James F. Digby, Rand Corp.; William Littlewood, American Airlines; Russell C. Newhouse, Bell Telephone Laboratories; and Nathaniel Rochester, International Business Machines Corporation. The task force was assisted by an "Ad Hoc Advisory Group" of scientists. See also *New York Times,* Nov. 13, 1961, and the Federal Aviation Agency, *Fourth Annual Report* (1962) and *Fifth Annual Report* (1963).

[8] Air Traffic Service, Federal Aviation Agency, *An Analysis of Project Beacon* (November 1961).

[9] *Washington Post,* Nov. 27, 1961.

[10] Federal Aviation Agency, *Fourth Annual Report* (1962), p. xv.

Meanwhile there had been internal management studies to guide maintenance systems (Project Searchlight), supply systems (Project Pipeline), and an external study by Harbridge House of contracting, procurement, and materiel functions.

All these studies were heavily oriented toward criteria of performance and efficiency. The question of economic worthwhileness was explored in a broad project begun just before the 1961 change of administration and finished in mid-1962.[11] An internal report the following year recommended broader and more systematic use of cost benefit analyses and establishment of a unit to do the necessary staff work.[12] The unit was not set up, and economic criteria continued to get less emphasis in FAA analytical work than had been recommended.

Variety of Technical Advances

The various task force recommendations, along with technical progress in both civil and military aviation, kept the agency's traffic and research and development experts moving ahead rapidly on different technical fronts. Even a partial list of matters that claimed their attention from 1961 to 1964 would include such complex and diverse enterprises as: [13]

Evaluating designs for supersonic transport planes

Working with the military on development of vertical and short-range take-off and landing ("V/STOL") aircraft

Installing a high-speed aircraft maintenance communication system

Studying reduction of air traffic control separation standards on North Atlantic routes

Developing lower cost instrument landing system ground equipment

Establishing a parallel instrument landing approach system

[11] Gary Fromm, *Economic Criteria for Federal Aviation Agency Expenditures* (United Research, Inc., June 1962, mimeo).

[12] Office of Policy Development, Federal Aviation Agency, *A Report on Benefit-Cost Analysis and Performance Measurement of the Air Traffic Control System* (April 1963, mimeo.).

[13] *Independent Offices Appropriations for 1965*, Hearings before a subcommittee of the House Appropriations Committee, 88 Cong. 2 sess., pp. 1105–11.

Modifying airway route structures
Completing the advanced radar traffic control system

Relationships with Military Aviation

One major effort that occupied FAA officials for several years
was Project Friendship, a plan for the agency to perform certain
aviation safety and traffic control functions for the Department
of Defense. The legislative history of the Federal Aviation Act
contemplated that air traffic control and towers, and other related
facilities at most Defense Department air bases, would come under
FAA operation and maintenance. After several months of attempt-
ing to pave the way for this change, in part through the creation
of a Federal Aviation Service, Halaby encountered serious Defense Department objections as well as misgivings within the FAA
and from its employee groups. A special interagency study group
then found that it would be uneconomic for the agency to take
over most of these facilities, largely because of the high salary cost
of FAA controllers. The Defense Department also determined
that it was no longer a defense requirement to establish a Federal
Aviation Service, and the study group recommended abandon-
ment of the pending Federal Aviation Service legislation. Although a number of Defense activities such as the operation of
Andrews Air Base Tower and the flight inspection of military air
navigation facilities were, in fact, transferred to the FAA under
other phases of Project Friendship, the consolidated civil-military
air traffic control agency envisaged by some of the supporters of
the Federal Aviation Act never came completely into existence.
Had Project Friendship proved feasible, some 10,000 to 15,000
employees would have been added to the FAA.[14]

Reaching Out to Constituents and the Public

The new Administrator gave fully as much energy and attention
to public relations as he did to program analysis. Even before he

[14] Letter to George A. Graham from Alan L. Dean, Associate Administrator for
Administration, Federal Aviation Agency, May 22, 1965.

was sworn in he began a series of strong personal efforts to win the support of aviation groups—flyers and businessmen whose goodwill toward FAA had sagged in the previous two years, as a stronger agency took charge and as decisions were bluntly made and defended by the forthright General Quesada.

Halaby sent out a "Dear Fellow Airman" letter asking the whole aviation community for help and ideas. He got back over a thousand suggestions, which were passed on for action to the appropriate divisions. A second letter then went to "fixed base" operators (those who run flying schools and provide general aviation services). This too solicited help and ideas and made a number of safety suggestions.

The Administrator also courted his constituents in person. He dedicated new airports, met with equipment manufacturers, and spoke to civic clubs. He sponsored a series of "Air Share" meetings in locations from Atlantic City to Alaska and Hawaii. At each one he outlined his own philosophy, answered questions, and listened to suggestions and complaints. He urged upon agency personnel the necessity of projecting an attractive public image, one which was "lean, clean, and keen"—a phrase replete with desirable objectives but sounding like television advertising at its worst.

Public relations as well as functional values were served by the design of new agency facilities. Offices were modern in design and emphasized use of open space and attractive colors. Halaby appointed an eminent and multi-occupational Design Advisory Committee to counsel him on this aspect of the FAA image.

The public relations and safety drives acquired a little "reverse English," but only temporarily, when a plane piloted by Halaby collided with another at Washington National Airport in a minor taxiing accident. The Administrator assumed blame and was fined fifty dollars by his own agency.[15]

New Organization, Too

Halaby took a fresh look at his organization as well as at his programs and his public relations. An internal organization study

15 *New York Times*, Nov. 10, Dec. 12, and Dec. 20, 1961.

had been made in 1959 recommending delegation of more authority to the regional offices. This proposal was shelved by Quesada, who believed in tight central administration and did not think that the agency had field executives who were ready to be entrusted with important delegations of authority. Halaby reversed this policy in a series of announcements in May and June 1961. Planning and policy-making were to be done in Washington, but field operations were to be directed from seven regional offices. Actual transition to the new plan began July 1, 1961, but was stretched out over about three years. Strong objections were raised by many of the employees scheduled for transfer from Washington to the field, but agency officials held firm, and the plan went into effect.

Organization below the level of the regional offices then became the subject of a unique experiment. The problem was how best to relate the work of traffic control centers, flight service stations, air traffic control towers, and other facilities to the regional offices. Under Project FOCUS (Field Organization Configuration Study) four experimental systems of organization were tried out in the field under controlled test conditions and under observation by a surveillance team from Washington. The project lasted about a year and culminated in a decision to adopt one of the four systems, the "comprehensive area manager plan." [16] Its final installation, after prolonged discussion with regional directors, was ordered in May 1965.

In the Washington headquarters the FAA operating bureaus were renamed "services" in 1961. A succession of changes during the 1961-65 period resulted in organization of most of the headquarters under three associate administrators, one each for administration, programs, and development. The regional offices were to report directly to the Administrator and Deputy Administrator, as were some special staff functions (medicine, policy development, law, general aviation affairs, information, appraisal, and international aviation).

Another innovation Halaby made soon after taking office was to

[16] Alan L. Dean, *The Federal Aviation Agency Field Organization Configuration Study (Project FOCUS)* (FAA, Sept. 25, 1964, mimeo.).

establish a management information center containing up-to-date charts on all important phases of agency operations, giving him what he called "a 360-degree view of the Agency." [17]

There are no absolutes by which to evaluate organization changes like those made in FAA but they "made sense." The Administrator decentralized the supervision of operations; he grouped headquarters functions into a logical pattern; and he arranged for specialized staff units to handle particular program areas.

The Top Personnel

The FAA personnel situation from 1961 to 1965 was not really stable; it was changing and developing.

Most of the changes in key personnel resulted from shifts in organization or from the creation of new services. Political patronage was negligible, and new officials were all technically qualified. One experienced official, interviewed late in 1964, said that the top officials could be divided into three approximately equal groups: old-timers from the Civil Aeronautics Administration, Quesada appointees, and Halaby appointees.

Halaby himself stayed in office until mid-1965. Also serving throughout this period were Alan Dean, Associate Administrator for Administration, and David Thomas, Associate Administrator for Programs, who had been head of the Air Traffic Service under both Quesada and Halaby. Deputy Administrator Pyle, as noted earlier, stayed till the end of November 1961. His successor— after a three-month gap—was Harold W. Grant, an Air Force general who had long commanded air traffic control and air communications services.

Halaby made very few changes immediately after assuming office. He did accept the resignation of James Anast, Director of the Bureau of Research and Development, whose relationships with other officials within the agency had not been smooth. The

[17] *Washington Post,* May 18, 1961.

job was then upgraded to Deputy Administrator for Development and filled by Robert J. Shank, an electronics expert with extensive industrial experience (Bell Telephone Laboratories and Hughes Aircraft).

Other opportunities were taken to strengthen the agency as its organization changed. The beefed-up regional director jobs were filled by some of the stronger veteran employees such as Arvin O. Basnight, former deputy to Dean; Oscar Bakke, former Director of the Flight Standards Service; and Joseph H. Tippets, who had been Director of the Bureau of Facilities and Materiel. Key technical operations were fortified by the assignment of some highly qualified men. Examples: the Deputy Administrator for Supersonic Transport Development, Gordon M. Bain, had been an official of the Civil Aeronautics Board and vice president of two airlines. The new Director of the Flight Standards Service was George C. Prill, an aeronautical engineer with experience in CAB and several airlines. Bernard J. Vierling, who headed the Systems Maintenance Service, also had airline experience and had managed his own aviation company.

Men with impressive experience also came into the management specialties. John R. Provan, the Veterans Administration's Assistant Administrator for Administration, was named Director of Management Services. Robert H. Willey became Assistant Administrator for Personnel and Training after service as Army's Director of Civilian Personnel and as Administrative Assistant to the Secretary of the Army. Other examples could be cited in other occupations, but the general personnel pattern was clearly one of knowledge and competence.

When Halaby resigned in 1965, the President nominated as Administrator General William F. McKee, retired Air Force Vice Chief of Staff. Thomas was then slated to become Deputy Administrator,[18] with Basnight moving in from the field to become Associate Administrator for Programs.

---

[18] General McKee's appointment required General Grant's resignation because the FAA Act says ". . . if the Administrator is a former regular officer of any one of the armed services, the Deputy Administrator shall not be an officer on active duty with one of the armed services or a retired regular officer or a former regular officer of one of the armed services." (72 Stat. 745).

The Budget and the White House

When Halaby took office he had to decide, as did all the new agency heads, what amendments to the Eisenhower budget should be submitted. He was reluctant to make drastic changes, but amendments were decided upon in three areas: (1) federal grants for airports, a subject on which the Kennedy administration was already committed to a change in policy; (2) financing of supersonic transportation studies; and (3) completion of Washington's Dulles International Airport.

In subsequent years agency expenditures and employment rose steadily to keep up with the increased volume of air transportation, but then leveled off with President Johnson's economy push in 1965 and 1966. The pattern of change looked like this: [19]

Fiscal Year	Actual Expenditure (in millions)	Actual Employment
1961	$638	42,838
1962	698	44,396
1963	726	46,313
1964	751	45,377
1965	769 (enacted)	45,100
1966	750 (est.)	44,430 (est.)

Many internal economies resulted from improved management systems installed after Halaby took office. Others, like planned economies in other departments, encountered political opposition. The Administrator told his House Appropriations subcommittee in 1964 that he was closing eight air route traffic control centers and forty-two flight service stations.[20] The closing of the flight service stations ran into congressional fire and was abandoned. An experimental program was substituted.

The trimming of the fiscal sails was one of two effects felt by the top FAA staff when President Johnson took office. The other was a lessening of the close relationship that Halaby had enjoyed with the White House. He had been, in effect, President Kennedy's

---

[19] Source: *The Budget of the United States Government* for the fiscal years concerned.

[20] *Independent Offices Appropriations for 1965*, Hearings, p. 1099.

personal aviation adviser. Nevertheless, there was no perceptible reduction of presidential support for the programs of the agency.

Change or Evolution?

Any evaluation of transition in the Federal Aviation Agency must acknowledge first that the task was less difficult than in the five cabinet departments already discussed. The agency is smaller (except for the State Department); its functions are narrower in scope; and the technical nature of its work is a partial buffer against political interference. Granting this, how much did the new administration transform the Federal Aviation Agency?

The officials interviewed agreed that from 1961 to 1965 there had been many changes, extensive changes. They pointed out, however, that most of the innovations resulted from the growth or maturation of the aviation industry, or from technological advances—rather than from differences in politics or policies. When air traffic increases, when speeds go up, when new radar gadgets are invented, the Federal Aviation Agency must change its activities, regardless of who is in charge.

One policy change was clear, but temporary. Quesada was phasing out airport grants, but Halaby increased them. Later, the Johnson administration decided to reduce the level of appropriations requested for this purpose.

Another clear difference was in organizational approach, but it may be argued that the agency had grown to the point where decentralization was inevitable.

There was no change of direction on most policy matters. Policies for which Quesada had fought, like compulsory pilot retirement at sixty and FAA control of "tall tower" obstructions, remained in effect. Work continued on the expensive and controversial designs for a supersonic transport plane.

Halaby did emphasize systematic analysis as a basis for policy change—analysis by competent groups drawn from various disciplines and organizations. He deserves credit also for care, clarity of purpose, and resolution in making organizational changes. And no new department head on the New Frontier worked harder than he did on public relations and client relations.

8 / EPILOGUE
How It Went--
And Can We Do Better?

> Fifty years ago on a Chicago streetcar I heard a woman
> explain to a child, "The President lives in the White House
> in Washington, where he signs bills they bring him, and he
> can do anything he wants to so long as they don't stop
> him."
>
> —Carl Sandburg
> Foreword, *To Turn the Tide* [1]

LIKE THE PRESIDENT, a new federal
department head "can do anything he wants to so long as they
don't stop him." Of course, he is stopped, or at least slowed down,
by many forces that restrict his freedom of choice. He is boxed
in by the detailed requirements of laws and regulations already
on the books, by the attitudes of his career staff, by pressures from
his constituencies, by congressional oversight, by guidance from
the White House, and by unforeseen events in the nation or
abroad. Despite these blocks and influences, he *can* change ma-
terially his department's legislative program and its method of
administration, as the preceding chapters have shown.

When a change of parties has occurred, there are indeed many
pressures that favor changes in policy. A sort of "governmental
Newton's law" takes effect. After an administrator has been saying
"no" for several years, his successor is under strong pressure from

---

[1] John F. Kennedy, *To Turn the Tide* (Harper & Brothers, 1962), p. xi.

his constituency groups to say "yes." The pendulum swings from more private power to more public power, from milder to stricter agricultural controls, from centralization to decentralization. Yet such influences merely favor change; they do not bring it about. The department head must exert driving effort to make changes— effort that is partly diverted and sapped by his newness in his job. Fortunately for the common defense and general welfare, however, he learns as he works. His endeavors to acquire information and to take charge are largely inseparable from his struggles to achieve his policy objectives.

How Good a Transition?

How did it go, then—this transition of six federal departments to the Kennedy-Johnson era?[2] As a basis for judgment, some standards can be suggested. In an effective change of administration the new political executives see to it that the program services and internal operations of their respective departments are maintained without serious sags or boggles; they come in with an understanding of key policy issues and with the main outlines of program plans to meet the issues; they are familiar within a short time with the resources, organization, key personnel, and functions of their departments; they avoid demoralizing the career staff; they are responsive to the President's program; and they work effectively with Capitol Hill and with their clienteles.[3]

On all these counts the transition went well. There were, of course, spots of delay, error, and confusion, but the total picture was of a successful take-over. Within weeks after Inauguration Day 1961, qualified men were fulfilling the responsibilities of the political jobs; legislative recommendations were sent to Congress;

[2] Caution should obviously be used in generalizing from the experience of five cabinet departments and one independent agency, even though they represent a large proportion of federal employment and federal expenditures.

[3] Readers interested in contrasting the 1953 transition with that of 1961 should refer to Herman Miles Somers, "The Federal Bureaucracy and the Change of Administration," *American Political Science Review*, Vol. 46 (March 1954), pp. 131–51; and Laurin L. Henry, *Presidential Transitions* (Brookings Institution, 1960), pp. 455–703, particularly pp. 467–87 and 639–703.

the "Eisenhower" budget was revised; analytical studies of programs and organization were started; and relationships were established with the various constituencies. No verdict should be ventured at this time on the quality of the total performance of the Kennedy and Johnson administrations, but there is no question that they assumed power effectively in these six organizations. Members of the new team in 1961 had charted the directions in which they wanted to go; they "lit running"; and there was no slackening of their pace. *Why* did the changes of administration go well? There are several reasons.

Plus Factors

First, and foremost, the new political executives brought to their federal jobs qualities that were effective in getting the administrations off to a good start. Some were "old hands" with high-level federal experience, like Secretary Rusk and many of his staff at State, and Assistant Secretaries Morris at Defense and Cohen at Health, Education, and Welfare. Others brought to their departments the right combination of attributes at the right time, like Secretary McNamara with his aggressive and analytical approach to management, and FAA Administrator Halaby, the public-relations-minded pilot and lawyer. Still others transferred political skills and experience to a new scene, like Secretary Freeman, governor of an agricultural state, and Secretary Udall, a congressman who had specialized on matters affecting the department he was to head. The heads of all six departments demonstrated high competence in both congressional relations and public relations.

There were cases in which some political executives did not "work out," but these were far fewer and less conspicuous than the successes. A few simply did not have the right combination of abilities to do the job demanded of them. Others were not compatible with their department heads. Still others became victims of political cross-currents. Only two or three "misfit" cases could be identified by the author in each of five of the departments studied. In the other, the Department of State, the number was greater, but this difference loses significance when one considers the Department's tradition of rotation in office and the enormous difficulties of formulating and administering foreign policy.

Perfection is never achieved in the selection process, and on the whole the secretaries and their staffs demonstrated effective competence and teamwork. Personnel stability at this level varied from department to department.

Second, President Eisenhower took a positive and constructive attitude towards the transition and instructed his administration to do likewise.[4] He behaved as if guided by Henry's prescription:

> The occupant of the White House cannot alone ensure a smooth transition to his successor. But in any given instance his conduct is crucial in getting the process started, reaching the right understandings with the other parties, and establishing a tone that will enhance the probability of the enterprise being carried through with dignity and statesmanship.[5]

The heads of the six departments all took their cue from the outgoing President and saw to it that their successors were well accommodated and briefed. Their personal attitudes ranged from partly concealed distaste (Interior) to hearty eagerness (HEW), but they were all helpful.

Third, the bureaucracies did their part effectively. The civil service officials in all six departments and members of the officer corps in the Pentagon, the Public Health Service, and the Foreign Service all responded cooperatively. Even allowing for their natural desires to protect their own interests and to make a good impression on their new chiefs, they performed well. They did many hours of extra work to prepare orientation material for the new political executives and they worked rapidly and conscientiously to meet the new demands for statistics, regulations, releases, and legislative messages in 1961. They responded equally well to the requirements of President Johnson's economy measures and task force studies in 1964. Many of the key figures in all this work had been through the 1953 transition and took the opportunity to improve upon it in 1961. On the whole, relationships

---

[4] See Chap. 1. Also, Laurin L. Henry, "The Transition: Transfer of Presidential Responsibility," in Paul T. David (ed.), *The Presidential Election and Transition 1960–1961* (Brookings Institution, 1961), *passim*.

[5] Laurin L. Henry, *Presidential Transitions*, p. 710.

between the New Frontiersmen and the bureaucrats were excellent.

Fourth, President-elect Kennedy adopted a brisk, "let's-get-started" attitude that was shared by his advisers. He responded appropriately to President Eisenhower's offers of aid, consulted with a wide variety of political and economic interests, and launched the "talent hunt."

Fifth, the "Kennedy task forces," particularly those that did their work before Inauguration Day 1961, helped formulate policies, evaluated potential candidates for jobs, and helped train them.[6]

Sixth, Capitol Hill received President Kennedy's nominees and messages in a cooperative spirit, although substantial action on many key proposals did not take place until after Johnson had become President.

Finally, the fact that the Democrats returned to power after only eight years' absence was unquestionably helpful. The Republicans in 1953 had been gone for twenty years and returned with an inexperienced team to a very different world of public problems. In 1961 a number of President Truman's staff came back to office. Also, most of the higher civil servants had been trained and conditioned in the Roosevelt and Truman administrations and made an easy readjustment to the New Frontier.[7]

And a Few Minuses

Effective as it was, the transition in these six departments could have been better. Delays and uncertainties could have been prevented if some of the political executives had been appointed earlier (for example, the Secretary of the Army, the Administrator of the Federal Aviation Agency). A more effective selection job could have been done in the case of others. Instances of strain from this cause have been noted in the earlier chapters on State, Defense, and Agriculture.)

Despite the generally agreeable psychological climate, there

[6] See Chap. 1.

[7] Over 90 percent of employees in grades GS-15 through 18, studied in 1963, entered federal service before 1953. See David T. Stanley, *The Higher Civil Service* (Brookings Institution, 1964), p. 24.

were also problems of relationships between career staffs and political newcomers. Earlier note has been taken of the morale problem in the State Department resulting from White House involvement in details of foreign policy, of anxieties among the military caused by Mr. McNamara's administration, and of civil servants in Agriculture wondering at first if Mr. Freeman was on their side. People feel threatened by change, and whether these relationships might have been handled better is a matter for speculation.

In some respects more change might have been accomplished. Nineteen sixty-one was a time when it would have been possible to take longer strides in tightening up organization and in modernizing management. The freshness of approach that characterized legislative and program changes penetrated into organization and management only in the Department of Defense—although the Federal Aviation Agency deserves honorable mention for its steps toward decentralization. Secretary McNamara understood that new methods of decision-making in the Pentagon could be adopted at the beginning of a new administration, and probably only then. The other cabinet officers discussed here were less management minded and apparently believed that they could attain their goals without drastic overhauls of structure or machinery.

It is normal for new secretaries to be more interested in program than in management and to postpone organizational and procedural changes. Yet if changes are to be made they will be easier if made at the start, and the new department head should have knowledgeable staff members ready to advance rapidly on the management front.

A Better System for Changes of Administration

The 1961 change of administration demonstrated that there is now an accepted pattern, or system, for making the change an orderly one. All three main parties to the transaction—the outgoing administration, the incoming administration, and the career staffs—planned and carried out their transitional responsibilities with ability and conscience. There were, inevitably, gaps and deficiencies.

Facilities and Expenses

Some of the salient problems were mundane but essential: expense money and facilities. President-elect Kennedy worked in his Washington home, his Cape Cod home, and his parents' Florida home. The pre-inaugural task forces, so important to the planning of the new administration, met in hotels, in Washington law offices, or anywhere they could. They had no government funds. For these and other transitional purposes the Democratic National Committee spent at least $360,000, and it was estimated that an additional $1 million of expenses were absorbed by the participants.[8]

Incoming cabinet and subcabinet officers were given space and secretarial help by their predecessors and in some cases were employed as consultants until they took the oath of office. These arrangements were made as the result of the goodwill of the Eisenhower team, not under a formally adopted general policy.

Both the absence of policy and the problem of facilities and expenses have since been remedied by the enactment of the Presidential Transition Act of 1963, whose statement of purpose is worth quoting in full:

> The Congress declares it to be the purpose of this Act to promote the orderly transfer of the executive power in connection with the expiration of the term of office of a President and the inauguration of a new President. The national interest requires that such transitions in the office of President be accomplished so as to assure continuity in the faithful execution of the laws and in the conduct of the affairs of the Federal Government, both domestic and foreign. Any disruption occasioned by the transfer of the executive power could produce results detrimental to the safety and well-being of the United States and its people. Accordingly, it is the intent of the Congress that

[8] *Presidential Transition Act of 1963*, Hearing before a subcommittee of the House Committee on Government Operations, 88 Cong. 1 sess. (1963), pp. 4–5.

appropriate actions be authorized and taken to avoid or minimize any disruption. In addition to the specific provisions contained in this Act directed toward that purpose, it is the intent of the Congress that all officers of the Government so conduct the affairs of the Government for which they exercise responsibility and authority as (1) to be mindful of problems occasioned by transitions in the office of President, (2) to take appropriate lawful steps to avoid or minimize disruptions that might be occasioned by the transfer of the executive power, and (3) otherwise to promote orderly transitions in the office of President.[9]

The act authorizes the Administrator of General Services to provide each President-elect and Vice-President-elect with space, staff salaries, travel expenses, authority to employ consultants, and other related necessities. It also provides for services and facilities needed by outgoing Presidents and Vice Presidents in winding up the affairs of their offices. Funds of $900,000 are authorized. This act is clearly a constructive step forward, as important for its policy declaration as for its detailed provisions.

Schedules and Messages

A related and much-discussed matter is the timing of the presidential election and inauguration. Proposals have been made, notably by Senator Mike Mansfield and Professor Paul T. David, that the inauguration take place earlier, thus shortening the period between election and inauguration.[10] The Senator proposed no change in Election Day but would move the inauguration to December 1. Professor David suggested that the election be held the first Tuesday in October, with inauguration the first Friday after the first Monday in November.[11]

[9] 78 Stat. 153.

[10] See summary of these issues in Laurin L. Henry, "The Transition: The New Administration," in David, *op. cit.*, pp. 264–67. Also see *Nomination and Election of President and Vice President and Qualifications for Voting,* Hearings before the Subcommittee on Constitutional Amendments of the Senate Committee on the Judiciary, 87 Cong. 1 sess. (1961), pp. 15–16, 426–30.

[11] One objective of these and kindred proposals not relevant to this discussion is to reduce the duration (and hence the strain and expense) of the presidential campaign.

Both proposals would give the incoming administration time and responsibility for preparing the State of the Union message, economic report, and budget message for Congress. The present practice of having these papers submitted by the outgoing President was called "silly" by President Eisenhower,[12] but these messages do have valedictory value and point up policy contrasts between old and new administrations. As Henry notes, the present practice "raises no overwhelming difficulties," and it would be undesirable to give the new President full responsibility for the budget but insufficient time to prepare it.[13] Both in 1953 and 1961 the present practice of having the budget prepared by the old team and amended by the new, worked well.

The proposition of shortening the election-to-inauguration period from two and a half months to one month is illuminated to some extent by the findings of the present study. Supporters of the shorter period say that an outgoing President has lost power, that decisions are delayed, and that a prolonged interregnum may be truly dangerous to the economy or the foreign relations of the United States.

One can debate whether the 1960-61 transition was a fair test of this view. It took place during a time in which reasonable domestic tranquility and prosperity prevailed and in which American foreign relations were seething but not erupting. There is no evidence to suggest that enemies foreign or domestic took advantage of the federal government during this period, but there is no assurance that they might not do so in the future. One can speculate that the Bay of Pigs error might not have been made by an administration longer in power. Undoubtedly some decisions were delayed and some proposals shelved when the election results were known. On the other hand the Eisenhower team was busy on relations with Cuba, the drain of dollars, new national monuments, and medical insurance proposals right up to the Inauguration Eve blizzard.

When this period is viewed as a time of preparation for the incoming group (as well as a time for winding up their previous work), it is scarcely long enough. Once a candidate is elected, he is almost overwhelmed by the people that must be seen, the

---

[12] Henry, "The Transition: The New Administration," p. 264.

[13] Ibid., p. 265.

plans that must be laid. In 1960-61, despite the organization of the task forces and the "talent hunt" and the brisk Kennedy pace, there were reports rendered and appointments made just before and even after Inauguration Day. If the pre-inauguration period is shortened, even more of the work of organizing the new administration will be done after inauguration, at the expense of actions that need to be taken by an informed and ready team. The only alternative is to steal time from preconvention and campaign activities to make some decisions on personnel and programs. Even confident candidates have not done much meaningful planning of their administrations before Election Day. All candidates should do more, but they are not likely to unless some major embarrassment or disaster in the future makes it very clear that earlier planning is absolutely necessary.

Whatever changes in schedule are made (and none seem likely at this time), the new administration must have time to get mobilized before it has to deal with Congress. This suggests strongly that there should be a period of at least forty-five days between the new President's election and the convening of Congress.

Personnel Changes Near the Top

The task of preparing for a new administration can be reduced and shortened if the President-elect will fill more of his appointive jobs from inside the government. Normal political pressures and his own inclinations will tend to keep him from doing so. Nevertheless, many well-qualified persons who can become assistant secretaries or agency heads are already working in the departments and agencies. They will be more sympathetic or adaptable to his policies than he realizes at the outset, and they will be invaluable in helping him get started.

Another personnel aspect of political change has been debated for years: How many jobs below the presidential appointee level should an incoming administration be able to fill with employees in whom it has confidence to carry out its policies? Officials of the Eisenhower administration, finding fewer jobs to fill in 1953 than they had anticipated, created "Schedule C," a category of confidential or policy-determining jobs exempt from the competitive civil service. There are now some 1500 positions in this group, but only a minority of the employees in these jobs are likely to be replaced in a transition. For one thing, more than one-third of these men are under the $10,000 salary level and are much less likely to leave than those in policy-making jobs.[14] Second, some employees in Schedule C have political or constituency connections of such formidable tensile strength that they stay in office regardless of which party has taken over the government. Third, others are seasoned professionals whose retention seems essential, as in the Department of Health, Education, and Welfare. Nevertheless, the exemption of selected high positions from the competitive service is a necessary way under present circumstances of giving an incoming administration opportunities to make replacements.[15]

More difficult and controversial is the question of what to do about high-level officials who are in competitive civil service jobs but whose attitudes or abilities do not meet the expectations of a new administration. The whole matter of tenure and flexibility of assignment in the higher federal civil service raises difficult dilemmas of equity and efficiency, as the extensive literature on this topic shows.[16] To make a long story short, the present situation is not satisfactory, and there must be some revision of civil service laws and regulations so that department heads have more freedom to replace or reassign higher civil servants without depriving them of career tenure, reducing their status and pay, or destroying their

---

[14] Thirty-four percent under grade GS-12, according to a special study of the data in *United States Government Policy and Supporting Positions*, Senate Committee on Post Office and Civil Service, 88 Cong. 2 sess. (1964).

[15] See discussions of Schedule C in transitions by Henry, in *Presidential Transitions*, pp. 727–30, and in "The Transition: The New Administration," pp. 248–50 and 263–64. Note also that there are other categories of non-civil service jobs that may be filled by an incoming administration. Again, see *United States Government Policy and Supporting Positions*.

[16] See particularly: Stanley, *op. cit.; Improving Executive Management in the Federal Government* (Committee for Economic Development, 1964); Paul T. David and Ross Pollock, *Executives for Government* (Brookings Institution, 1957); and Commission on Organization of the Executive Branch of the Government, *Personnel and Civil Service* (1955), pp. 37–44; and the Commission's *Task Force, Report on Personnel and Civil Service* (1955), pp. 49–62.

prestige. If this is done the pressure to exempt positions from the competitive civil service will be greatly reduced.

Effective Transitions of the Future

The Eisenhower-Kennedy transition was good. It contained most of the necessary features of an effective transfer of power. The transitions of the future can be even more effective if the executives involved build on the experience of the past and if they take full advantage of the Presidential Transition Act of 1963. It will be necessary, of course, for both the incoming and outgoing administrations to carry out the full spirit of the act and to take the appropriate actions in a timely and cooperative manner.

The outgoing President should again set an example of friendly consultation and should "pass the word" that incoming political executives are to be given the facilities and information they need. He should again direct the Bureau of the Budget to stimulate and coordinate preparations for the changeover, to be responsible, in effect, for agenda for the transition. It may or may not be advisable to use impartial outside help in these preparations, as was done in 1961. The outgoing President is more likely to do his part in making the transition effective if he is retiring from public life. If he is a defeated candidate his cooperativeness with the incoming group will depend upon the history of the campaign, upon his own philosophy, and upon his personal relationship with his successor.

The President-elect, well before he knows he is the President-elect, should begin planning for the programs and personnel of his administration. Once elected, he will again need a central liaison representative (like Clark Clifford in 1961) to deal with the White House staff. He will also be well advised to use policy study groups on the model, if not the scale, of the Kennedy and Johnson task forces. He will most certainly need a new "talent hunt" effort —and the effort should be as intensive inside the government as outside. He will also find it advisable, as President Kennedy did, to hold over a few of the preceding administration's political executives (1961 examples: York in Defense, Pyle in Federal Aviation,

Dominy in Interior) in places where this will be helpful to his programs. He should also make it clear by precept and example that administrative assistant secretaries and other key civil servants will be relied on for studies, arrangements, and advice; they will respond.

No transition, no matter how it is systematized or funded, will work amid incompetence, distrust, or ill will. The 1961 change of administration in these six departments went well because it involved first-rate men working in a positive spirit. Future transitions *can* be even better. They can also be worse, particularly if personal feelings have become bitter. Yet there is more ground for optimism than pessimism. The success of 1961, added to the successful aspects of the 1953 transition, has fostered a constructive attitude toward the transfer of power. The citizen can hope that all parties to future changes of administration will make the further changes and devote the extra effort needed to assure that power will change hands with a minimum of risk and confusion.

Index

Achilles, Theodore C., 25-26

Administration (*see also* Management; Organization): Agriculture, 91; Defense, 43-44, 47, 49-52; Federal Aviation Agency, 122; HEW, 106; Interior, 71; State, 13, 27-31

African nations, relations with, 4n, 9, 10, 19, 26

Aged, aid to (*see also* Medicare), 99, 101, 103-04, 111

Agency for International Development, 22, 29, 111

Agricultural Economics, Bureau of, 88-89

Agriculture, Department of, 78-96

Ailes, Stephen, 53

Air Force, 35-36, 44, 49, 51-52, 56

Air transportation, 114-19

Aircraft. *See* Bombers; Carriers; Supersonic transport plane

Alliance for Progress, 20

Altschul, Selig, 117n

Ambassadors, 19-20, 25

American Farm Bureau Federation, 88, 92

Analytical planning: Defense, 36-44; Federal Aviation Agency, 117-20, 126

Anast, James, 123

Anderson, Clinton, 63

Anderson, George, 54

Andre, Louis E., Jr., 118n

Ankeny, M. J., 63

Appalachia program, 113

Armed forces (*see also* Air Force; Army; Navy), 32-34, 38, 46, 48

Arms Control and Disarmament Agency, 23, 28

Army, 35, 44, 47, 49-50; Reserve, 55-56

Assistant secretaries: Agriculture, 62n, 79, 84-85; Defense, 34-36, 47, 50, 52-54, 62n; HEW, 62n, 98; Interior, 62; State, 17-21, 62n

Bagwell, John C., 84

Bain, Gordon M., 124

Baker, John A., 79, 84, 90

Bakke, Oscar, 124

Balance of payments, 4n, 10

Baldwin, Claude, 86

Baldwin, Hanson W., 57n

Ball, George, 8, 13, 17, 20, 21, 27; Ball-Sharon task force, 10-11, 19

Ball, Robert M., 107, 110

Barnes, Carl B., 87

Barry, Frank J., 63

Basnight, Arvin O., 124

Battle, Lucius D., 18, 30

Bay of Pigs, Cuba, 23, 25, 64, 135

"Beacon" project (FAA), 117-18

Beasley, D. Otis, 62, 75, 86n

Benson, Ezra Taft, 82, 83, 86-88, 93

Berlin, 9, 12, 23

Bernstein, Marver, 86n

Bertsch, Howard, 86

Betts, Ernest C., 87

Bombers, 2, 37, 38, 54

Bonneville Power Administration, 68, 76

Borklund, C. W., 50n

Bowles, Chester, 8, 13, 16-17, 20

Brady, Nyle, 90

Briefings, 130; Agriculture, 82; Defense, 34-35; Federal Aviation Agency, 116; HEW, 100; Interior, 65; State, 12-14

Briggs, Frank, 62

141

PRINTED IN THE UNITED STATES OF AMERICA
BY GARAMOND/PRIDEMARK PRESS, INC., BALTIMORE, MD.